Plant propagation in pictures

For J. H. BEALE and H. E. DOWNER
my classmates at the Royal Botanic Gardens, Kew, England,
and my best friends.

The author standing before a Garland Butterfly bush (*Buddleia alternifolia*) started from a cutting six inches long ten years previously. See page 106.

Plant propagation in pictures: HOW TO INCREASE THE NUMBER OF PLANTS IN YOUR HOME AND GARDEN BY DIVISION, GRAFTING, LAYERING, CUTTINGS, BULBS AND TUBERS, SOWING SEEDS AND SPORES.

ILLUSTRATED STEP BY STEP WITH MORE THAN THREE HUNDRED AND FIFTY PHOTOGRAPHS AND ELEVEN LINE DRAWINGS.

MONTAGUE FREE

THE AMERICAN GARDEN GUILD, INC.,
and DOUBLEDAY & COMPANY, INC.,
GARDEN CITY, NEW YORK, 1957

Books by Montague Free

Gardening
All about House Plants
All about African Violets
All about the Perennial Garden
Plant Propagation in Pictures

Library of Congress Catalog Card Number 57-6709
Copyright © 1957 by THE LITERARY GUILD OF AMERICA, INC.
All Rights Reserved
Printed in the United States of America
Designed by Joseph P. Ascherl

Preface

This book is for amateur gardeners. It is designed to aid those who
have no special facilities for plant propagation but who are interested in the processes involved and who may want to increase
their stocks of certain favorite plants. Although it is primarily a
"picture book," it is desirable to read the Foreword and also the
introduction to each chapter.

My sincere and hearty thanks go to my long-suffering wife.
Without her help you would have had to wait at least another
year before seeing these lucubrations.

Contents

Preface   7

Foreword   11

I   Seeds and spores   17

II   Vegetative or asexual propagation   53

III Propagation by cuttings   78
     Conventional methods   78
     New and unusual methods   138

IV   Bulbs, corms, tubers, rhizomes, rootstocks   155

V   Runners, offsets, stolons, and suckers   177

VI   Layering   183

VII Perennial vegetables   195

VIII Graftage   198

IX   Rooting mediums and equipment   220

     Appendix   232

     Index   239

     Acknowledgments   251

Foreword

THE PROPAGATION OF PLANTS. The most intimate friend of my boyhood happened to be the son of the head gardener of a large private estate, and through him I became interested in the mysteries of plant propagation at a very early age. He showed me that it was possible to root the side shoots removed from Tomatoes when pruning them to a single stem; and that young Apple trees could be produced by planting the pips from the apples we shared. (All too often my share was the core, so I had plenty of seeds with which to experiment!) In one respect both of these bits of information were misleading. Tomatoes are not usually propagated by cuttings, because it is more advantageous to raise them from seeds; and Apples are not raised from seeds, excepting understocks for grafting and when the production of new varieties is desired, because the characteristics of the parent may not be reproduced in the seedlings. On the other hand, the information so casually acquired led to the knowledge that there are at least two methods whereby plants can be propagated—sexually, by seeds and spores; and asexually by vegetative parts of the plant.

For more than fifty years I have been concerned, more or less, with various aspects of plant propagation and at divers times have held the position of propagator in three extensive establishments. But, even now, when birthdays roll around with appalling frequency and they are viewed with alarm rather than with delight, plant propagation—the miracle of the germinating seed, the rooting of cuttings, and the successful union by grafting of two diverse plants—has lost none of its power to provide the thrill of accomplishment. This little bit of autobiography is introduced to indicate the enduring interest conferred by a knowledge of plant propagation.

Everyone who maintains a garden practices plant propagation to a certain extent, even though it may be no more elaborate than scattering seeds of annuals in the places where they are expected to bloom. But, sometimes, raising plants from seeds is not so simple as this, for certain seeds require special handling to ensure satisfactory germination. This may involve: the removal of the pulpy covering, cracking, filing, abrading, or otherwise treating the seed coat to allow the moisture to penetrate to the embryo; stratification in a moist medium to enable the seeds to retain their viability; storing in low temperatures to bring about certain changes in the seed essential to germination; the provision of high or low temperatures according to the subject; the right light conditions and, in some cases, excision of the embryo. A knowledge of the various factors influencing germination is of immense value to the gardener whether he be amateur or professional.

There are some plants which do not come true from seeds. A knowledge of the various ways of vegetative propagation enables us to increase our stock of these plants by division, cuttings, grafting, or budding, methods which as a rule ensure the perpetuation of the desirable characteristics (and also unfortunately, the undesirable ones) of the parent plant.

It may be maintained that these specialized methods belong in the province of the professional—the nurseryman and the florist. This is true, in part, but, as will be seen later, there are many occasions when it is desirable for the amateur to do his own propagating, and knowing how is essential.

In nature plants propagate themselves sexually by seeds and spores; asexually (vegetatively) by bulbils, bulblets, corms, cormels, tubers, rhizomes, runners, offsets, suckers, stolons, layers, divisions, and cuttings.

It may be asked how on earth plants can make cuttings of themselves, and it must be admitted that the term is not literally accurate, but in effect it is true enough. The twigs of some Willows (which form roots with greater ease than those of any other tree) are so brittle that they become detached as a result of windstorms or by birds lighting on them. Furthermore some species of Willow prune themselves annually by developing what is known as an abscission layer at the base of some of the twigs. (An abscission layer is a zone of corky cells similar to that which enables the leaves of deciduous trees to fall off in the autumn.) As almost everyone knows, the natural habitat of many Willows is along riverbanks and some of these broken-off twigs fall into the water, are carried downstream, and some, becoming lodged on a mud-bank, take root, and thus a new tree is started.

Plant propagation in pictures

CHAPTER I

Seeds and spores

SEEDS are infinite in variety, in size, and in shape. Some are infinitesimally small: such as Begonia, one ounce containing about a million seeds; in contrast the Double Coconut, the largest known seed, may weigh upward of fifteen pounds. In shape they vary from the spherical, shotlike seeds of Canna to the curious angular seeds of the Brazil Nut, and the winged seeds characteristic of the Catalpa and the Empress Tree (Paulownia).

In texture they may be soft, as in the cases of Ismene and Crinum, whose seeds may be easily picked to pieces by a fingernail, or extremely hard as in the Ivory-nut Palm, which has been used as a substitute for ivory.

The leaves of seedlings of some plants are very different from those of mature plants. In some cases, if these seedlings are propagated by cuttings before the adult foliage is formed, the juvenile habit is retained. An example of this is to be found in Retinispora varieties, which are juvenile forms of False Cypress (*Chamaecyparis*) and Arbor-vitae (*Thuja*).

The primary purpose of seeds is to ensure the perpetuation of the species and in many cases Mother Nature has devised means whereby they are widely distributed. There are some which have *parachutes,* such as the Dandelion, Milkweed, and Salsify; there are *gliders,* such as Maple, Pine, Birch, and Empress Tree; *floaters in water,* which include Sea Coconut or Double Coconut and Water Lily; there are *aerial floaters,* which have cottony appendages such as do the seeds of Willow and Poplar; other air-borne seeds include many of the Bromeliads and Orchids; then there are the *hitchhikers,* such as Burdock, Beggars Tick, and the interesting Unicorn-plant. The fruit of the last-named has a long curved horn, which, when mature, splits into two curved grappling hooks. Several of these are produced in a ring surrounding the fruiting stems, which lie upon the ground, so that when a horse or similar animal steps in the middle of a clump, the hooks become engaged by the hair of the fetlocks and thus may be distributed over a large territory. Squirrels and birds (bluejays in particular), in their endeavors to provide food for themselves during the long winter, also are responsible for planting seeds of Oak, Walnut, and Hickory when they fail, as they often do, to find the seeds which they have so carefully hidden. Sunflowers, also, may be inadvertently distributed by birds. Here at my home, "Buttonwoods," every year Sunflowers come up in odd places, doubtless from seeds dropped by chickadees or nuthatches after they have visited the bird feeder.

You, too, probably help to disseminate seeds when you come in contact with a clump of Burdock, Beggars Tick, or Galium, whose hooked fruits or seeds cling to clothing as well as to the hair of animals. There are some whose fruits are *explosive,* such as Squirting Cucumber, Witch Hazel, and Legumes such as Scotch Broom. Then there are the *sprinklers,* such as those of the Poppy and the East Indian Lotus. There are many fruits which are attractive to birds, such as those of the Honeysuckle, Holly, and Turquoise Berry. These have pulpy coverings which are digested by the birds and the hard seeds are evacuated, unharmed and with a modicum of fertilizer.

Seeds

More flowering plants are produced from seeds than from any other means. Usually seed germination presents no problem to the gardener, provided that the seeds are given their minimum requirements of air, moisture, and sufficiently high temperature.

These requirements are met in outdoor planting by covering the seeds with soil deep enough to keep them moist, but not so deep that they do not get sufficient air, or so deep that the food stored in the seed is exhausted before the growing shoot reaches the surface.

Temperature requirements are met either by starting the seeds in a greenhouse or in the home (if you have a well-lighted window in a cool room—60° to 65°), in a hotbed or a cold frame; or by deferring planting until the ground is warmed up sufficiently in the spring. Many seeds succeed best in cool temperatures and some can advantageously be planted outdoors in late fall. These will germinate in the early spring when the temperature is right for them. Some of the *hardy annual* seeds, such as Love-in-a-mist, Annual Larkspur, Shirley, and California Poppies, may be planted in late summer or early in the fall so that they germinate and form young plants which are capable of surviving the winter. These plants usually bloom early and last longer than those from spring-sown seeds.

Biennials such as *Althaea rosea* (Hollyhock), *Bellis perennis* (English Daisy), *Campanula medium* (Canterbury Bells, *C. medium calycanthema* (Cup-and-saucer Bells), *Cheiranthus Cheiri* (Wallflower), *Dianthus barbatus* (Sweet William), *Digitalis purpurea* (Foxglove), *Lunaria annua* (Honesty), *Myosotis* (Forget-me-not), *Verbascum olympicum* (Greek Mullein) and *Viola tricolor hortensis* (Pansy) are sown from June until August.

Late April or early May is the best time for sowing most of the *hardy perennials,* although the early bloomers which ripen their seeds before August can, to advantage, be sown as soon as they are ripe. The seeds may be sown in a prepared seed bed in the open, although it is preferable to have some kind of transparent or translucent cover to avoid the danger of heavy rain.

Except for those perennials with a mixed ancestry, as a result of the efforts of the plant breeders, which cannot be relied on to come true, raising from seeds affords the gardener a ready means of quickly increasing his stock. The named varieties of genera such as Phlox, Peony, Chrysanthemum, when grown from seeds, usually produce progeny mixed in character, with the chance that most of them will be inferior to the parent. On the other hand, there is a bare possibility that some of the offspring may be better. Among the plants which can be satisfactorily raised by seeds are the following: species of Columbine such as *Aquilegia caerulea* and *A. chrysantha,* assuming that there are no other Columbines nearby, which could be mixed with them as a result of the ministrations of bees or hummingbirds; Plume Poppy (*Bocconia cordata*), Coreopsis, Bleeding-heart, Gas-plant (Dictamnus), Christmas-rose (Helleborus), Gay Feather (Liatris), Perennial Flax (Linum), Lobelia, Balloon-flower (Platycodon).

Cattleya Trianaei—capsule and ripe seeds. I have not counted the number of seeds, but my guess is that they exceed a million.

Here is a member of the Pineapple family whose capsules have just opened to display the seeds waiting for a puff of wind to blow them away. This is an epiphyte, or "tree percher." Those seeds that lodge on a moss-covered trunk or branch are likely to grow.

The soft fleshy seeds of Ismene germinate when they are ready, regardless of moisture. The seeds pictured here started to grow in September while in an ash tray on the author's desk.

April 3, following year. On the right is a seed that germinated and made roots when placed on moist soil in a terrarium. The one to the left was kept in the ash tray and is living on its own "fat." Notice that the seed is wrinkled owing to the withdrawal of nutrients.

May 6. The seed has disappeared. The plant has made a small bulb and the beginnings of a leaf. It should be planted outdoors in fairly rich soil as soon as danger of frost is past.

Unicorn-plant (Proboscidea), showing the vicious hooks which may become tangled in the hair above the hoof of a horse who happens to step on it. In this way the seeds may be distributed over an area covering several miles. Incidentally, I have read somewhere that the owners of horses in "Proboscidea countries" detest this plant because of the injury to horses which may be brought about by the constant irritation of these grappling hooks.

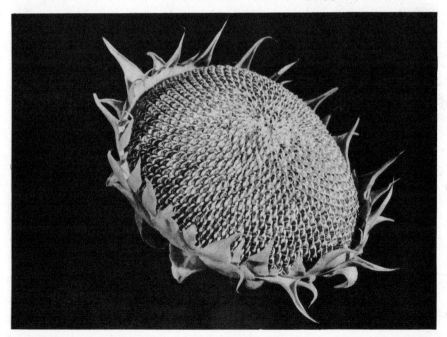

Sunflower seeds are favorites of many seed-eating birds. In our garden every year Sunflowers germinate as a result of seeds which nuthatches, bluejays, and chickadees inadvertently drop.

Fruit of Magnolia in various stages. Notice the seeds, which have a pulpy covering. These are eaten by birds, the pulpy covering is digested, and the seeds are evacuated unharmed.

Salt-shaker-like fruits of the Oriental Poppy. Seeds are spilled out of the holes beneath the cap by action of wind or by an animal brushing against the stems when they are dry and brittle.

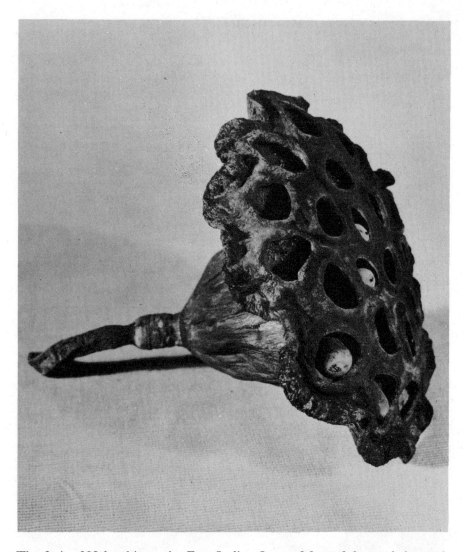

The fruit of Nelumbium, the East Indian Lotus. Most of the seeds have already fallen out from this specimen. These drop into the water and may float for a considerable distance before they sink into mud at the bottom of the pond.

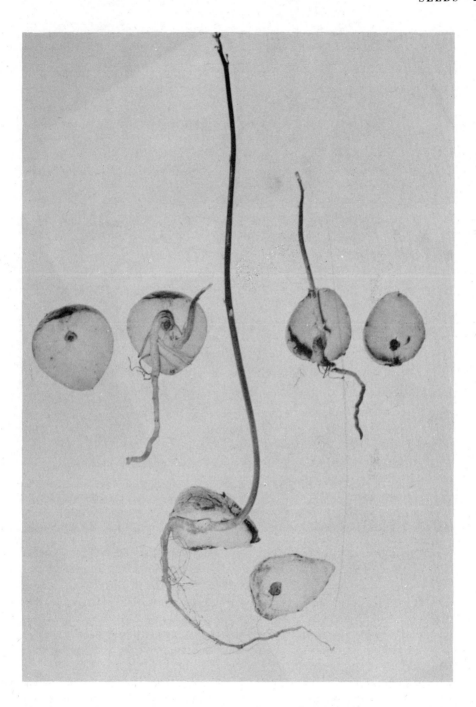

The seeds of Avocado germinate no matter whether the seeds are planted with the pointed end up (the right way), on their sides, or upside down.

Sowing seeds indoors

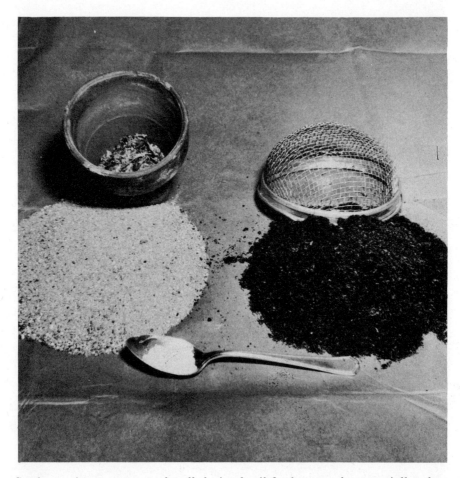

Seeds require a porous and well-drained soil for best results, especially when they are sown indoors. The standard soil mixture for seeds in general consists of equal parts of loam (garden soil), leaf mold and/or peat moss, and sand. See pages 220 to 223 for soil-mixture pictures. Here you see a flowerpot with drainage in the bottom and equal parts of sand, rotted compost, and peat moss suitable for Saintpaulia (African-violet), Begonia, Gloxinia, etc., which thrive on it. In the spoon there is a small quantity of pulverized limestone to neutralize the acidity of the peat moss. The strainer with ⅛-inch mesh is used to provide an extra-fine layer on the top of the seed pot. It can also be used as an aid in covering the seeds when this is necessary.

This mixture minus the limestone is suitable for acid-soil plants such as Rhododendron and Mountain-laurel. See page 224, Sphagnum Moss.

Preparing the soil. A good way to ensure that the soil is not too loose or packed too tightly is to fill the pot with moist soil, not wet, not dry, tap it on a bench or table, strike off surplus soil so that it is level with the pot rim, and then press it down, or firm it, about a half inch below the rim. Firming can be done by means of a tamper like the one pictured (left), which was made from a section of a tree branch about 2 inches in diameter, or you can use the bottom of a drinking glass.

Under no circumstances should you "puddle" the soil. The photograph on the right demonstrates the bad effect of "puddling." Corn was seeded in both of these pots and received exactly the same treatment with measured amounts of water. The only difference was that the soil in the pot which shows no growth whatever was puddled by stirring it when it was wet, thus driving out air. This explains the often-reiterated advice: "Do not attempt to work on the soil when it is wet."

Sowing the seeds. No attempt should be made to cover small seeds such as those of Begonia and Saintpaulia (African-violet); merely gently press them into the surface with a tamper.

The pot can be covered with glass or plastic film, which should be removed as soon as germination is evident.

A white-seed variety of Lettuce was chosen to illustrate the ideal spacing for seeds of this size.

Because Lettuce seeds are supposed, under some conditions, to require light for successful germination, these were covered with a very thin layer of sand. Ordinarily the rule to follow when planting seeds indoors is to cover them with soil equal in depth to twice the diameter of the seeds.

There are two methods of moistening the soil. One is to stand the pot in an inch or two of water and leave it there until moisture shows on the surface.

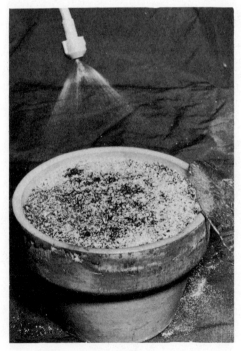

Another way is to use a fine spray.

One means of germinating small seeds, such as Begonia, Gloxinia, and Saintpaulia, is in square Mason jars. Enough finely screened soil is put in a jar to bring it to the top of the shoulder and is pressed down with a knife blade.

There are two ways of introducing the seeds into the jar. One is by means of a knife blade on which the seeds are placed.

The blade with the seeds is carefully inserted into the Mason jar and by tapping it gently against the side of the jar the seeds are evenly distributed.

Another and perhaps simpler way is to put the seeds in an iced-tea spoon, holding the handle in one hand and lightly tapping the spoon with the finger of the other hand. After the seeds are sown, the top is then put on the jar without any rubber ring. This will largely prevent loss of water by evaporation and at the same time permit interchange of air. The only advantage these methods have over the orthodox way described on page 28 is that, if the soil is sufficiently moist when it is put in the jar, it will remain that way until seeds have germinated and are large enough to be transplanted.

When the seeds have germinated and are large enough to be pricked out (transplanted), they can be removed with the aid of a teaspoon.

Handling small seedlings such as these is facilitated by the use of a "transplanting fork," which can be made from a 6-inch wooden pot label by cutting the pointed end to a sliver and then making a notch in it.

Although the orthodox soil mixture in which to start seeds is equal parts of sand, garden soil, leaf mold and/or peat moss (right), there are some gardeners who prefer a sterile medium such as vermiculite (left).

It is necessary, however, when a sterile medium is used, to provide nutrients for the seedlings. This is the same flat of seedlings after two applications of a soluble commercial fertilizer to the vermiculite section.

Rebutia minuscula (Echinocactus minusculus) Flat of seedlings in orderly array.

Seedlings of *Cereus Spachianus.* Before the young plants become too crowded in the seed pot or flat, they should be transplanted.

Orchids

Raising Orchids from seeds used to be a gamble (Some will say that it still is!), up to 1903, when Noel Bernard demonstrated that mycorhiza fungi were necessary to ensure the development of Orchid seeds. This was a great improvement over the haphazard method that prevailed previously. About twenty years later Dr. Lewis Knudson of Cornell University showed that it was possible to germinate sterilized Orchid seeds in flasks, on a sterilized nutrient solution of agar; thus proving that fungi were *not* essential to germination. Essential are: (1) use of a nutrient solution containing cane sugar plus mineral salts; (2) great care to do the work under aseptic conditions.

If you are interested in raising Orchids from seeds, I would suggest that you consult *Home Orchid Growing,* by Rebecca Northen, Van Nostrand, N.Y.; or *Orchids Are Easy to Grow,* by H. B. Logan and L. C. Cosper, Ziff-Davis Publishing Co., New York.

From seed pod to flowering plant.

Sowing seeds outdoors

One of the first requisites for sowing seeds outdoors is the preparation of a fine seedbed. This is accomplished by first digging up the soil, breaking up the lumps, and then raking the surface, removing stones and trash in the process. When very small seeds are to be sown, such as those of Poppy or Portulaca, they are sown directly on the raked surface, which is then patted down with the end of the rake. See page 38. Seeds may be broadcast; or sown in rows, drills, or furrows.

If the soil contains so much clay that it is heavy and sticky, avoid planting seeds when it is wet, as this may result in puddling the soil to such an extent that air is driven out and the germination of the seeds thereby is prevented.

The soil in a small area, such as that enclosed by a cold frame, can be modified by adding a 3-inch layer of sand and an equal amount of peat moss or sifted leaf mold. These should be dug into and thoroughly mixed with the upper 3 to 4 inches of the natural heavy clay soil. This should be done several weeks ahead of planting in order to give the soil a chance to settle. Or, provided it is not too wet, it can be consolidated by tramping.

In order to make a shallow drill a rake is used, keeping one foot on the line to insure that the drill is straight.

Seeds may be sown directly from the packet. It is essential to sow them evenly and thinly. For example, the seeds of Sweet Alyssum should be spaced about 1 inch apart.

The seeds are covered by raking across the drill, and then the soil is firmed down by patting it with the head of the rake.

The best tool for making a furrow for reception of larger seeds is a draw hoe. Notice that the right foot of the operator is kept on the line to prevent it from being pushed out of position, which would result in a curved row.

Seeds are sown thinly or thickly according to the subject and the objectives in view. In the case of vegetables, such as peas, that are destined to mature without any transplanting, the aim is to have an ultimate space of about 2 inches between the plants. Therefore seeds are sown about 1 inch apart to take care of loss of seeds by failure to germinate. On the other hand, if the seedlings are to be transplanted, spacing may be a little closer.

Covering the large seeds may be done as shown on page 38, but some prefer to do the covering with their feet by shuffling along the row in such a way that the seeds are covered and pressed down at the same time.

Trees and shrubs from seeds

Those which have comparatively large seeds, such as Ash, Oak, Linden, or Euonymus, can be planted in the open ground just as soon are they are available. These should have a covering of soil equal in depth to two or three times the diameter of the seed.

Those species of Maple which ripen their seeds early in the year, also Willow and Poplar, are short-lived and must be sown as soon as they are ripe. Chestnut, Oak, and Walnut lose their vitality if they are allowed to become thoroughly air-dry. Therefore, these also must be sown or stratified as soon as they are ripe. Stratification is the name applied to the practice of putting seeds in layers (strata) in a moist medium such as peat moss, sand, sawdust, or a mixture of these. It is usually considered more desirable to mix the seeds throughout the medium, but the name still stands.

Seeds which have fleshy coverings, such as those of Apple, Cotoneaster, Barberry, Dogwood, Holly, and Rose, should have the pulp removed before they are planted.

There is a group known as "two-year seeds," which ordinarily do not germinate for two years or more after planting. They include some of the Roses, Hawthorns, and Cotoneasters. A convenient way of handling these, together with those mentioned above, is to put them, mixed with peat moss, in small jars which are covered either with glass or with plastic film such as is used in the freezer. The seeds should be placed in such a way that some of them are visible from the outside. The jars should be put in the family refrigerator and looked at from time to time. As soon as any signs of germination are apparent, the seeds should be removed and planted in a regular soil mixture of equal parts loam, sand, and peat moss or sifted leaf mold.

Small seeds, such as those of Hemlock, Spruce, Fir, Larch, and other conifers together with Philadelphus (Mock-orange) and Spirea, may be kept dry, preferably under cool conditions (50° to 60°), during the winter and sown in the spring. These usually can be handled most effectively by sowing them in either flats (shallow boxes about 3 inches deep) of any convenient size, usually about 12 by 18 inches, or small pots.

Rhododendron, including Azalea and other acid-soil plants, such as Enkianthus, Leucothoë, Oxydendrum, Heath, and Heather, can be sown in Sphagnum (see page 224) or in a mixture of sand and peat moss or Oak leaf mold. Ordinarily no attempt is made to cover these small seeds with soil. However, some gardeners prefer to put a very thin layer of dry Sphagnum rubbed through a fine-mesh sieve—a piece of metal fly screening can be used—or you can borrow your wife's flour sifter. The necessary moisture is maintained by putting on a glass or plastic cover, which should be removed as soon as the seedlings appear.

Usually it is necessary to keep the small seeds under cover to avoid any danger of their being washed away as a result of heavy rain. A cool greenhouse is ideal for starting them, but if you don't have a greenhouse, you can improvise one for pot-sown seeds by plunging the pots in peat moss in an apple box, which should be covered with a sheet of glass or plastic film fastened to a wooden frame.

Once the seeds have been sown, it is necessary to keep the medium moist. This can be done by means of a fine spray or by standing the pots or flats, temporarily, in water about 1 inch deep, which will be absorbed by capillarity. Just as soon as moisture appears on the surface, they should be removed from the water.

Except for shade-loving plants, when the seedlings are up they should be given all the sun available.

Berried trees and shrubs

Usually it is desirable to remove the pulpy covering of certain seeds such as Holly, Viburnum, and Cotoneaster before stratifying or sowing them. This can be done by putting the berries in water and leaving them for a few days until the covering is soft and easy to remove.

The strawberry-like fruits of Kousa Dogwood are being soaked in water to soften the pulpy covering.

Here the seeds are in process of being removed from the fruits with the aid of a household strainer.

The seeds were put in moist peat moss on November 2 and placed in the family refrigerator, which is kept at approximately 40°. The white arrow is pointing toward two of the seeds.

On January 31 they were removed from the refrigerator and placed on the shelf in my study. Signs of germination were evident on February 11. They were photographed on February 13. The next step is to transplant them.

Holly Berries at left; seeds with pulp removed at right. There are usually about four seeds in each berry.

These can be sown in wooden flats, first treated with a preservative such as copper naphthenate (Cuprinol), either broadcast (left) or in rows (right).

The seeds are then covered with about 1 inch of soil, sand, or, as is done here, with vermiculite.

Excision of the embryo

Even though it requires considerable skill on the part of the operator, it is desirable to say something about this method of propagation. Excision (cutting out) of the embryo has been successfully used to hurry up the germination of "difficult" seeds. Not only is it a means of inducing the seeds to germinate, but it also increases the rate of growth of the seedlings. For example, it is possible to bring Roses into bloom the same year the seeds are produced. Irises have been grown to blossom stage in less than one year instead of the two or three years that are required normally.

Two Crab Apple seedlings, each one year old, which were planted the same day. The small one, on the right, was planted in soil; the larger seedling, left, the excised embryo was planted in a test tube.

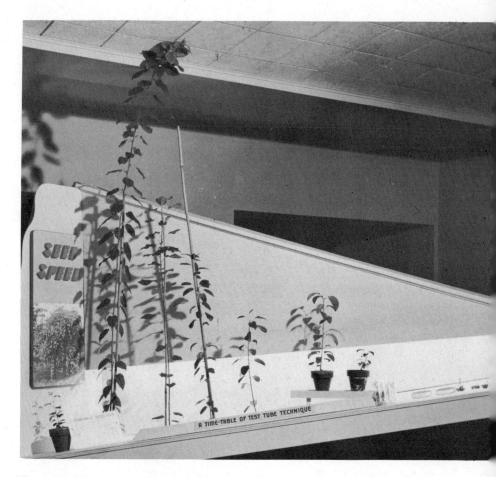

The stages in seedling development using embryo-culture techniques. From right to left: Crab Apples form mature tree; sterile Petri dishes in which embryos are excised from the seeds; test tubes containing young seedlings; progressively larger seedlings. At far left is a seedling from a seed planted in soil on the same day that an embryo was planted in a test tube, which resulted in the seedling second from left.

EMBRYO CULTURE
OF CRABAPPLES

TRANSPLANT
TO SOIL

CRABAPPLE
FRUIT
SINGLE
SEED
EMBRYO
3 DAYS
5 DAYS
1-2 WEEKS
2-3 WEEKS
3-4 WEEKS

Drawing showing the weeping Crab Apple fruit, cross section of the fruit, seed, embryo, and stages in the development of the embryo in sterile culture. When seedlings have reached the stage at the extreme right, they are transplanted to soil in 2-inch pots.

It is necessary to remove the embryo under aseptic conditions. The surface of the seeds is sterilized by soaking them in a water solution of calcium hypochloride. The embryos are then removed with great care, by using sterilized razor blade and dissecting needle. The room in which the work is done may be sprayed with 1-per-cent solution of carbolic acid to reduce the danger of contamination by air-borne bacteria and mold spores. The embryos are then carefully planted in jars containing sterilized nutrient agar. The foregoing merely outlines the bare bones of the processes involved. If you are interested enough to want to try embryo culture, you should acquire a copy of the *American Iris Society Bulletin,* May 1945.

Spores

Although as far as the gardener is concerned there is little difference between seeds and spores, botanically they are vastly different. A *seed* is the result of the fertilization of an egg cell in the ovule by its union with the sperm cell from a pollen grain. When mature it contains a plant embryo surrounded by seed coats. A *spore* in many cases, as in ferns, is a specialized cell which under suitable conditions germinates to form a prothallus, which on its underside produces male elements (antheridia) and female elements (archegonia). Spermatozoids produced in the antheridia swim by means of vibrating cilia in the film of moisture usually present on the underside of the prothallus, and unite with the egg cells produced in the archegonia. The result is the fertilized egg cell (oöspore), which is perhaps more nearly comparable to a seed. The fertilized egg cell goes through a process of segmentation which finally leads to the development of a plant similar in appearance to the fern which produced the spore.

Asplenium ebenoides (Scott's Spleenwort), a hybrid between the Walking Fern (*Camptosorus rhizophyllus*) and the Ebony Spleenwort (*Asplenium platyneuron*) possesses some of the characteristics of both parents—its fronds tend to root at the tip, as do those of the Walking Fern; and they are partly pinnate, showing the influence of the Spleenwort. The parentage of the hybrid was suspected for a long time and finally was demonstrated by Miss Margaret Slosson—presumably by sowing spores of both species in the same germinating medium. In Alabama it is more abundant than elsewhere, and is believed to be self-perpetuating there.

We don't hear a great deal about Fern hybrids, even though they are not uncommon. They may occur when two species are growing in close enough proximity to enable their spores to be distributed and mixed in the same area. If the sperm of one species happens to wander into the archegonium of another species, a hybrid may result.

It is easy to raise Ferns from spores. All that is necessary is to "first catch your hare" or, in other words, first get your spores. These usually are produced on the undersides of the fronds. They require close watching, using a hand lens, if necessary, to see when the spores are ripe, which occurs when the spore cases begin to split open. When this is seen, the frond should be removed and placed on a piece of white paper. By the following morning, in all probability, the paper will be discolored by millions of spores.

A good way to plant these is to secure first a common brick, on the upper surface of which should be spread a layer of sand and sifted leaf mold or peat moss. This can be put in the oven for about one half hour at 250° to sterilize it. Carefully remove the brick and put it in a vessel containing about 2 inches of water. A plastic breadbox serves admirably for this purpose. As soon as the soil is obviously moist, spores can be scattered on the surface. This method can also be adapted to sowing very small seeds, such as those of Begonia, Gloxinia, and Saintpaulia.

Though happy in the limestones of Bartholomew's Cobble (Sheffield, Mass.) and similar locations, the charming little Walking Fern (*Camptosorus rhizophyllus*), so named because of its lengthened frond tips, which root to form new plants, is difficult to establish, often simply walking into oblivion.

Ebony Spleenwort (*Asplenium platyneuron*) is a delightful little Fern, easy to transplant into the shaded rock garden. It and the Walking Fern are the parents of *Asplenium ebenoides,* a true bigeneric hybrid, which occurs only infrequently.

Scott's Spleenwort is intermediate between the two parents, with fronds that have a tendency to form plantlets at the tips; notice the one at the top left-hand corner.

Fern prothallia and seedlings of Saintpaulia. If you are wondering why the Saintpaulia happens to be mixed in with Ferns, it is because, as my wife insists, I am a pessimist. You see, the Fern spores were planted first and nothing happened for a long time, so I decided that they were not viable and sowed Saintpaulia seeds, which promptly germinated along with the spores.

CHAPTER II

Vegetative or asexual propagation

THIS is a term applied to the propagation of plants from parts other than seeds or spores. They may consist of stems, leaves, roots, or, rarely, of fruits (Prickly-pear Opuntia). Propagation may be effected by division of the rootstock, by cuttings, or by graftage. In general, plants raised by asexual propagation reproduce the parent plant exactly, but there are a few exceptions to the rule. If leaf cuttings are made of the Snake-plant—*Sansevieria trifasciata Laurenti*, the variety whose leaves are marked with yellow longitudinal stripes—the progeny lacks the yellow stripes, possibly because they revert to the original species. Some varieties of Pelargonium (House Geranium), notably the one known as Mrs. Gordon, when propagated from stem cuttings, have white flowers tinted with pink, but, when raised from root cuttings, they have deep red flowers. A similar phenomenon is seen in the case of the variety of Bouvardia known as "Bridesmaid," which has pink flowers when propagation is by stem cuttings, but, when raised from root cuttings, the flowers are deep red. One cannot always rely on Saintpaulia (African-violet) varieties to come true from leaf cuttings. Sometimes three distinct color forms, "blue," white, and pink may originate from a single leaf.

The understocks used in budding and grafting also may exert an influence on the size of the varieties which are grafted on them. Malling IX, for example, is well known as a dwarfing understock for Apples.

During the last five or ten years there have been considerable changes in techniques, especially in connection with cuttings, in such matters as wounding the stems by cutting through the bark or by inserting them in an abrasive medium such as powdered glass.

Polythene, a plastic film permeable to air but retentive of moisture, has been put to good use in air-layering and also as a covering for cuttings.

Constant mist, a technique by which wilting is prevented by keeping the leaves almost constantly moist under a mistlike spray, is a valuable means of propagating certain plants.

Division

Division is among the surest and easiest methods of plant propagation. It is applied almost exclusively to herbaceous plants—especially the hardy kinds. The most important thing to remember is to do the job at the right time. This occurs when the plants are dormant, in spring or fall. A good general rule to follow is to divide early-blooming plants in the fall and late blooming ones, such as hardy Asters and Chrysanthemums in the spring. There are a few exceptions: Primroses can be divided immediately after the flowers fade, in the spring before growth starts, or early in the fall; the Bearded Irises July to September; Oriental Poppies and Madonna Lilies should be separated when the foliage becomes yellow in August.

Greenhouse and house plants are best propagated by division, when possible, in the spring, when their new growth is about to begin.

When only a few plants are needed, divisions can be set where they are to remain, with care taken, however, to ensure that the soil does not become dry. If a large number of plants is desired, as, for example, when Japanese Irises are separated into single shoots (which involves considerable root injury), the divisions should be set in a special plant bed in which the soil has been made porous by the addition of sand and peat moss. It may be necessary to shade them from bright sun until they begin to grow and it is especially helpful to put them in a cold frame covered with a sash for a few weeks.

House plants

In all cases involving severe root disturbance it is desirable that the pot should be well drained. The usual way of doing this is to put a piece of broken pot over the hole in the bottom and then about ½ inch of smaller pieces.

A plant of Saintpaulia in need of division.

Five rooted divisions were obtained from this specimen.

This shows a three-crown plant in process of being divided.

The divisions are potted in 3-inch pots.

Two pots of *Saxifraga sarmentosa*. The one at the left is a plant with several crowns, one at the right is a "single-crown" plant. (See also Chapter V.)

This plant has been turned out of its pot and is in process of being divided.

In this picture you see the results. It won't be long before they look like the single-crown plant in the rear.

Ferns such as this (*Polystichum tsus-simense*) often become root-bound, so division is necessary. Start the process by cutting into the root ball with a knife.

Then separate the crowns, as is shown here. When the division is made for propagation purposes, they can be divided into many more by cutting or pulling them into pieces, each having a single crown.

In this case only two plants were desired.

Here is a Snake-plant (see also page 129) capable of being divided to make several plants.

A good way to do this is to stick two hand forks back to back into the root ball to pry it apart.

In this case four for one were obtained.

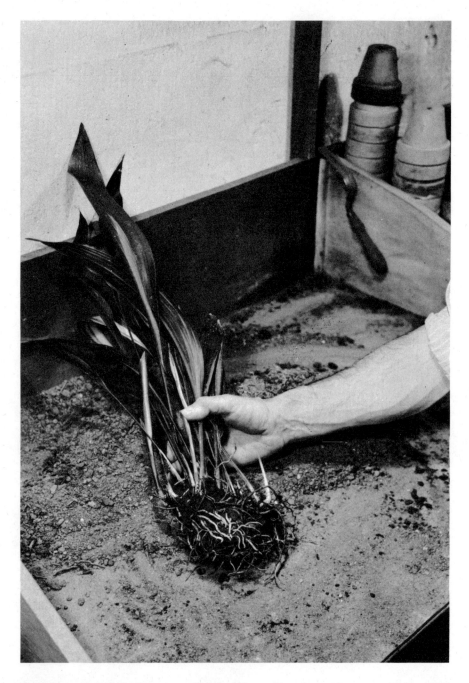

Aspidistra, sometimes known as Saloon-plant, Cast-iron-plant, can be handled similarly to the Snake-plant. The one you see here could be divided into several plants, each one with a leaf and a growth shoot.

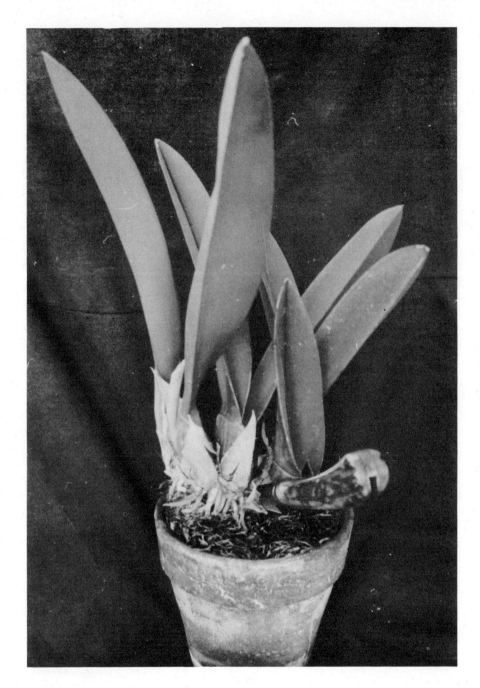

Orchids can be propagated by division by utilizing the "back bulbs." Often it is desirable to separate them a year ahead of the time when the actual division is done, by cutting through the rhizome.

Here you see a new shoot originating from the back bulbs of *Oncidium tigrinum*.

The time to do the dividing is soon after the flowers fade and when the new growth is about to start.

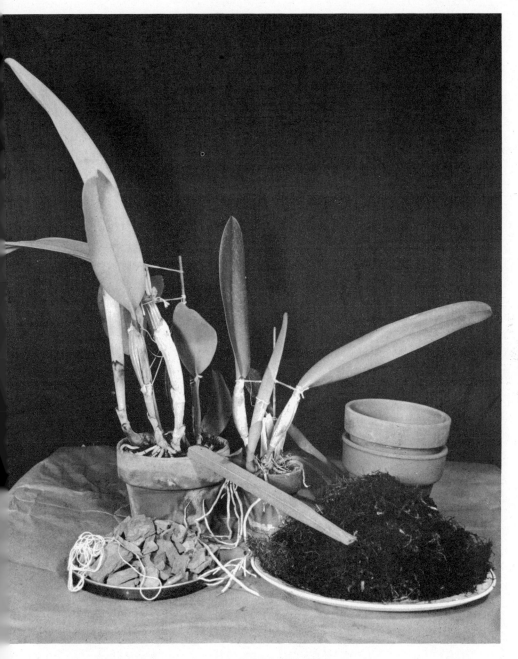

The "makings" needed for potting orchid divisions are shown here; soft string for tying the pseudobulbs to a wire stake; crocks (broken flowerpot) used for drainage; a potting stick with which the osmunda fiber is firmly packed around the roots; and clean porous clay pots.

Most orchids require good aeration at their roots. Therefore, sometimes it is desirable to increase the size of the drainage hole in the bottom of the pot. This can be done by tapping gently around the hole with a hammer.

When the division is removed from the pot, dead roots are cut off.

The pot is prepared for planting by filling it one third full of crocks as a further aid to aeration and drainage.

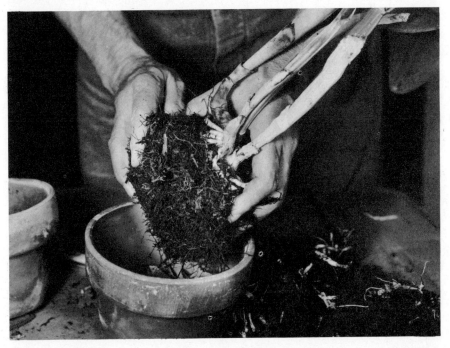

A wad of moist osmunda fiber is then wrapped around the roots. (Moist osmunda is easier to handle than dry. The day before it is to be used it should be dipped in water and then allowed to drain.)

Put the division in the pot with the oldest part touching the rim. This, in most cases, enables the growing point to be centered. Additional osmunda fiber is then packed in firmly between the roots and the side of the pot.

A wire stake is put in and the pseudobulbs are tied to it.

Stray "whiskers" of osmunda fiber are trimmed off with shears.

Hardy herbaceous perennials

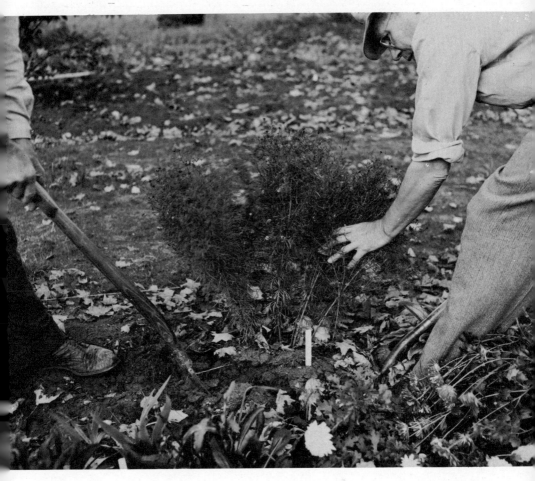

Coreopsis tinctoria (Golden Shower) being dug up preparatory to division.

A good way to start is by prying the clump apart with two spading forks placed back to back.

The hole to receive the division is made with a spade and should be large enough to contain the white shoots and the roots without crowding.

The fibrous root system of Day-lily requires a somewhat different technique. A clump is dug up preparatory to dividing.

Pushing through the clump two spading forks, back to back and close together to pry apart the root stock, is preferable to chopping the clump with a spade.

Further division into pieces of planting size is done with a hand fork. In some cases they can be pulled apart with the hands. The divisions should be reset at the same depth as they were before digging them up.

Ordinarily this plant of Hosta, or Plantain-lily, would be considered a good size for planting.

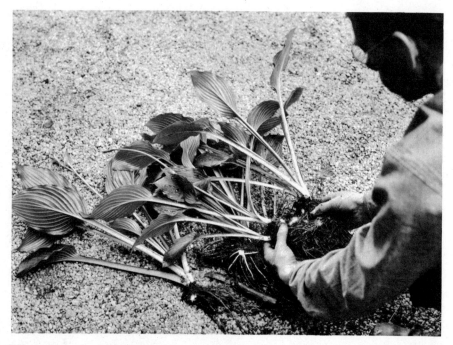

When you are thinking in terms of propagation, the plant can be divided as seen here.

Here is a clump of Lily-of-the-valley dug up in the fall and divided as shown under *Coreopsis tinctoria*.

Pieces of suitable size ready for planting. If rapid propagation is needed, they could be separated into individual shoots with the roots attached.

The first step in propagating Peonies by division is to dig up the entire plant and shake the soil away from the thick, fleshy roots. If the soil happens to be sticky and clayey, it may be necessary to wash it off with a hose.

Some three- to five-eyed divisions can be pulled off with your hands. Others must be cut apart.

Here the clump has been divided into three- to five-eyed pieces. One of these divisions has only one eye. Small pieces such as this are desirable only when division is done primarily to increase the number of plants.

When planting the divisions it is essential that the soil be firmly tamped to prevent future subsidence. None of the eyes is more than 2 inches below the surface.

When the Peony division is set at the right depth, fine topsoil is put in between and over the roots so as to be in full contact with them. Tramping will then pack the soil firmly to eliminate all the subsurface air pockets. Be sure to cut off the stubs of the stalks to lessen the danger of attack by botrytis disease.

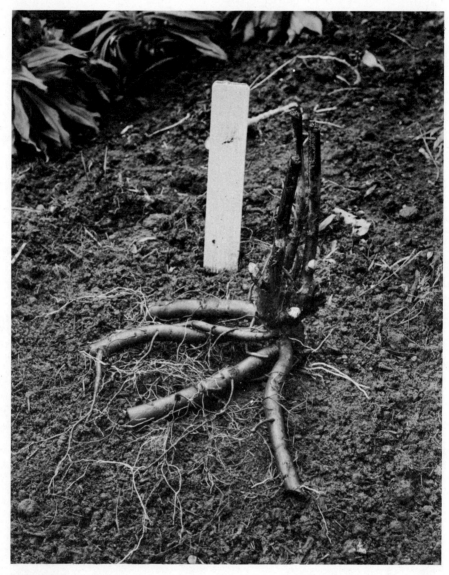

A division dug up about six or eight weeks after planting shows the new roots, the white fibrous ones, which have already started to grow.

September is the best time to divide Peonies because the soil is warm enough to encourage formation of new roots, which lessens the danger of "heaving" as a result of alternate freezing and thawing during the months ahead.

When dividing Phlox, dig up the entire plant and pry strong pieces from the outer edges of the clump with a hand fork. The worn-out center (note the thin spindling stems) should not be used for propagation purposes unless absolutely necessary.

The divisions should be planted in holes large enough to contain the roots without crowding. Cover them with soil and pack it firmly around them, either with the hands, as shown here, or with the feet, as shown under Peony.

Polyanthus can be divided as soon as the flowers have faded, provided that the divisions can be planted in a partly shaded position and can be watered during dry spells. If these conditions cannot be met, it is better to defer the dividing until the fall or early the following spring. In this picture you see a plant being dug up.

The clump is divided by separating the crowns.

The divisions are planted by making holes with a trowel.

Three plants obtained by separating have been planted and are being watered. Notice that the flower stalks have been removed to divert the energy of the plant from seed production.

CHAPTER III

Propagation by cuttings

CONVENTIONAL METHODS

Stem cuttings of house plants

Although these can be rooted indoors at almost any time, June, July, and August are preferred for most of them because young plants of good size are developed before it is necessary to bring them indoors before frost. Another advantage is that the propagation can be done outdoors.

The simplest way to raise house plants from cuttings is merely to dibble them in outdoors in a shady spot. Usually early August is the best time to do this. Here you see Iresine (also known as Bloodleaf), Patience-plant, and Begonia.

Campanula isophylla, the Ligurian Harebell (sometimes erroneously called Star-of-Bethlehem), is often grown as a house plant, although when suitably located outdoors it can endure temperatures down to zero.

Cuttings should be made in the spring, when it is possible to obtain short, stocky growth from the base of the plant.

The cutting is inserted in the standard sand, soil, and peat-moss mixture (1 part sand, 1 part peat moss, 1 part garden soil), surfaced in this case with vermiculite. If more convenient, sand can be used instead.

Cutting is placed in a polythene bag. Ordinarily it is not necessary to close the top of the bag, but under very dry air conditions it is better to do so.

Eight weeks later the cutting is a well-rooted plant.

This shows the method of making the basal cut of the House Geranium. Notice the position of the thumb of the right hand, which supports the cutting without the danger of slicing into it. (My wife and daughter say I'm way off in this!)

A 3-inch pot is filled with standard seedling and cutting mixture, a hole is made with the blunt end of a pencil, and a little sand is poured into the bottom of the hole. This provides the free drainage which is desirable.

The cutting is then inserted and the soil is pressed down firmly around about it.

Cuttings of (left to right, top to bottom) Fuchsia, Abutilon, Patience-plant, Wandering Jew, and Coleus.

These can be inserted in a bulb pan filled with standard soil mixture and surfaced with a layer of sand. When a hole is made with a dibble, a little sand is carried to the bottom. In this picture the method of making the soil firm about the base of the cutting is shown.

A shoot of Lantana prepared for insertion. The undesirable portions, leaves, immature seed heads, and flowers encircle the cutting.

Lantana—the result obtained from the preceding.

Stem cuttings of *Echeveria microcalyx*. These can be inserted directly in a flat containing the standard mixture. They do not need any covering.

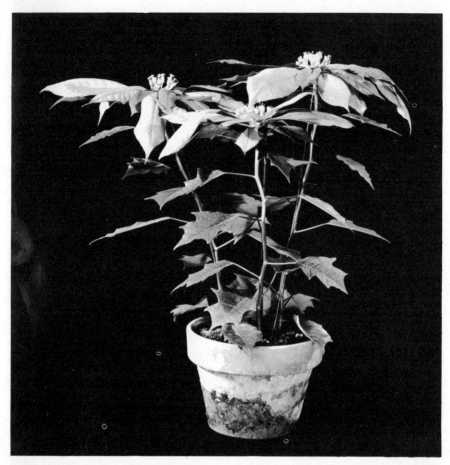

Poinsettia. Usually when Poinsettias are grown in the house, large plants are not desirable. The way to insure this is to take tip-shoot cuttings in August, obtained from a plant received at Christmas and kept dry in the cellar from February to May.

How to pot a Poinsettia cutting.

DIBBLE HOLE

SAND

SOIL

POT CHIPS

The cuttings of Poinsettia, about 6 inches long, may be inserted in 4- or 5-inch pots of the standard 1-1-1 mixture, putting a handful of partly rotted manure in the bottom of the pot and a layer of sand on the surface. The top of the plastic bag is rolled down to facilitate the insertion of the pot. Then it is rolled up and fastened with a rubber band.

You can expect something like this five or six months later.

Three scrawny house plants, left to right, Impatiens, Coleus, and Vinca. They have no claim to beauty in their present condition.

Here they are again, with the material suitable for cutting removed. Beauty is still conspicuous by its absence and it would be better to discard them. In the foreground there are cuttings at the left of each plant; leaves, debris, and flowers at right.

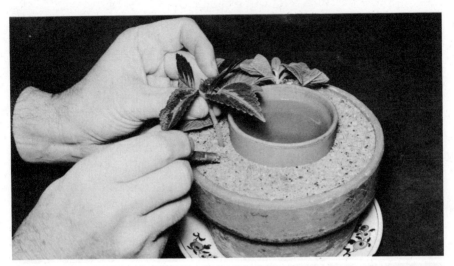

This is a "Forsyth" cutting pot. It consists of a 6-inch bulb pan in which a small porous clay pot is centered. The drainage hole of this pot is plugged either with cork or chewing gum. This pot is kept filled with water. After the initial watering the seepage from the central pot usually is sufficient to keep the rooting medium moist.

In the dry air of the average living room it is helpful to enclose the potted plant within a plastic "tent"; or you can use cellophane, as was done in this case.

Multiple-crown plant of Saintpaulia (African-violet) Plants with single crowns usually are preferable.

The surplus crowns can easily be removed by cutting them with a sharp knife—a kitchen paring knife will serve.

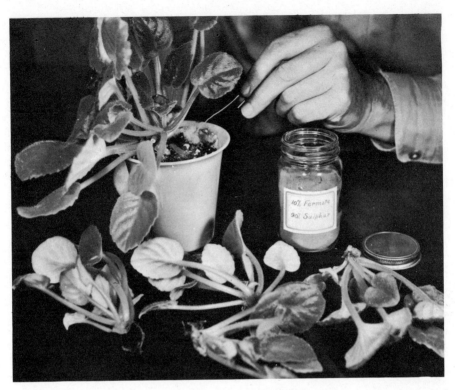

Four crowns have been taken from the original plant. The wounds are dusted with a fungicide. The "duster" is a small piece of lamb's wool attached to a straightened-out paper clip. The severed crowns can be planted in the standard cutting mixture. They should receive extra shade for a week or two, by which time they should be able to withstand the normal light for Saintpaulia.

Often diseases can be by-passed by rooting cuttings of non-affected parts. One such is the crown rot which sometimes affects Saintpaulias.

The affected part has been cut away.

A good way to root crowns such as this is to put them in a saucer of water. After a few weeks enough roots are formed so that transplanting is necessary.

One of the difficulties encoun-
tered when transferring water-
rooted cuttings to soil is that the
roots cling together when they
are removed from water.

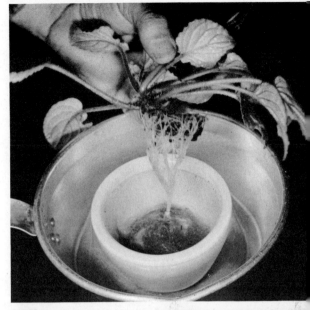

This can be overcome by putting
the new container in a pan of
water, which enables the roots to
spread out naturally.

Pour in the soil while the roots
are still submerged. The soil
should be filled in level with the
pot rim and the plant taken
from the pan of water. The soil
can be made sufficiently firm
merely by tapping the pot bottom on a bench or table.

Screw-pine (Pandanus) is an excellent house plant when it is young and has an undivided crown, but the time usually arrives when they become too large for their location and are cluttered with surplus shoots. These can be taken off, the cuts made as near as possible to the parent stem.

The so-called "bedding plants," some of which have already been discussed (House Geranium and Lantana), can be included here. Alternanthera (which can also be divided), Echeveria, and Lobelia are examples.

About one third of the top growth should be removed by shortening the leaves.

The trimmed shoot is inserted in sand in a 3-inch pot with the rooting medium packed firmly around the base of the shoot.

This is then covered with a small glass jar or tumbler; or by poly-thene plastic such as used for freezer wraps.

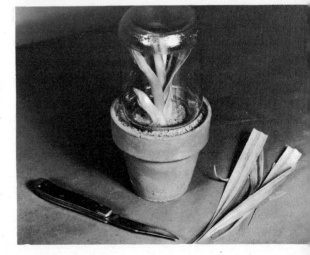

Softwood cuttings of hardy shrubs and trees

GENERAL CARE

A humid atmosphere must be maintained about the cuttings, which means that the frame or case should be kept closed most of the time and the cuttings sprinkled occasionally. It is a good plan to ventilate the frame by tipping the sash for a half hour or so every morning, and on hot, humid days a crack of ventilation may be left all day. The rooting medium must be kept constantly moist. Bottom heat is desirable but not necessary. See pages 230–231.

Shade from bright sunshine is necessary in our climate, but ample light is essential. The frame may be placed in the shade of a building or a large tree. In the open I have had good success by whitewashing the underside of the glass and providing an additional covering, for use when the sun is bright, of a double thickness of cheesecloth attached to light wooden strips cut to fit the frame; or lath shades could be used.

Yellowing and fallen leaves should be removed daily. When the cuttings have rooted (in three to nine weeks or longer), they should be dug up and potted or planted out in another frame, where they must be shaded for ten days or until they become established in their new quarters. They can be transplanted to the open the following spring.

Timing

A start can be made with softwood cuttings of *Neillia sinensis* in mid-May, continuing with Lilac at the end of the month. However, June and July are the big months for this kind of propagation. Lilac cuttings, for example, should be put in soon after the flowers have faded in late May or early June; some, as you will see if you consult the Propagation Notebook in the Appendix root very well from mid-June insertions; but I would be willing to take a chance with most shrubs in July, including Azalea, Barberry, Boxwood, Forsythia, Daphne, Diervilla, Hydrangea, Tamarisk, Spirea, Viburnum. Some, such as evergreen Barberries, Chamaecyparis, Juniper, Mahonia, Pieris, Rose,

Thuja, and Viburnum, are likely to give a better percentage of rooting if they are inserted toward the end of July or early in August. Don't be deterred from trying cuttings of any kind if you feel like it, but I should warn you that Cryptomeria, Magnolia, and large-leaf evergreen Rhododendrons are all likely to be disappointing.

The differences between softwood, half-ripened wood, and mature wood cannot be defined with any accuracy. Softwood cuttings are those taken early in the growing year before the growth is finished for the season. Mature wood is that at the end of the season of growth, usually in September and October. The half-ripened wood is that which comes in between, say in July and August.

Softwood cuttings of shrubs and trees

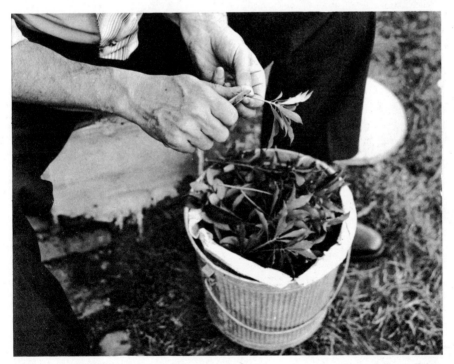

When making softwood cuttings it is desirable to prevent them from wilting. If you have a variety of cuttings which have to be collected from a considerable distance, wilting can be prevented by carrying them in a container lined with wet newspaper—in this case a garbage pail was used.

A variety of cuttings ready for insertion. Left to right, top row: Wisteria, Rose, Lilac, Boxwood; bottom row: Bush Honeysuckle, Pieris, Garland Butterfly-bush (*Buddleia alternifolia*), and Winter Jasmine (*Jasminum nudiflorum*).

Two sections of cold frame are being prepared for reception of the cuttings. Underdrainage is important. If the soil does not naturally drain, it is necessary to excavate to a depth of 6 inches or so and fill it with coarse sand or gravel. The dark-colored medium is a mixture of sand and peat moss. On the right is coarse sand.

The sand and, to a lesser extent, the peat moss and sand should be packed down firmly. Here a half brick is being used.

With a strip of builder's lath to serve as a guide the cuttings are inserted and made firm, with particular attention paid to the base of the cutting by pushing the dibble in from the side.

When two or three rows have been put in, they are thoroughly watered, which helps still further to consolidate the sand.

The cold frame sash is then put in place. Shade is necessary to prevent the temperature from rising too high. This can be done by painting the underside of the glass with whitewash or by putting on a covering of cheesecloth, double or triple thickness, or both. It may be necessary to ventilate by raising the sash on hot, humid days.

This is a homemade propagating frame with a window sash for covering.

When only a few cuttings are to be inserted of each kind, usually it is better
to put them in pots.

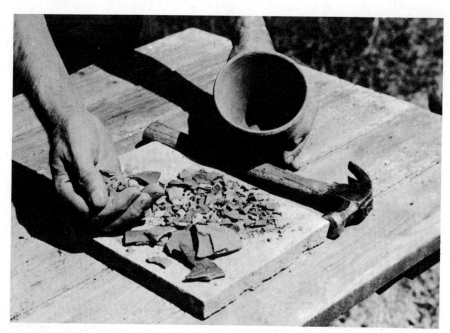

It is desirable to put extra drainage material in the bottom of the pot.

The big advantage of inserting the cuttings in pots for hardening off is the easy removal of those which root ahead of the others.

Summer cuttings of *Euonymus Fortunei vegetus*. These easy-to-root plants can be started by inserting them in a mixture of sand and peat moss. They should be kept in a shaded cold frame with the sash on until they are rooted. Roots are produced more freely in some media than in others. These two groups of cuttings were inserted at the same time, the batch on the left in a 50-50 mixture of peat moss and sand, while those on the right were rooted in a mixture of equal parts of sand, good garden soil, and leaf mold.

Cuttings with strong roots should be potted up immediately. Here a cutting is being potted individually in a 3-inch pot in a mixture composed of equal parts of soil, sand, and leaf mold. Be sure to provide proper drainage at the bottom and to water the cutting thoroughly after potting it up.

Those to the left (*Euonymus Fortunei vegetus*) were potted singly late in summer. Those to the right, including Buddleia, Kolkwitzia, Symphoricarpos, and *E. kiautschovica*, were left in the original pots. All were carried over winter in the cold frame and plunged to the rim in sand. After a few hard frosts they were covered with a deep blanket of hardwood leaves and the sash was put on the frame.

The following spring a line is stretched; a trench is made to receive the bare-root cuttings.

A trowel is used for planting the potted-up cuttings, a method equally applicable to planting cuttings directly from the cutting pot. The line has been removed simply to get it out of the way. First, however, a marker furrow was made to ensure a straight row, which makes routine cultivation simpler.

The roots are slipped into the trench and the soil is pushed firmly against them with the fingers. Be sure to leave plenty of room between cuttings so that both root and top growth can continue undisturbed, without competition, until the shrubs are big enough to go into the garden or to final locations.

Three years later *E. kiautschovica (patens)* has attained a stature of 3 feet.

Similarly, Garland Butterfly bush (*Buddleia alternifolia*), Beauty-bush (*Kolkwitzia amabilis*), and *Symphoricarpos Chenaulti* range from 3 to 4 feet. These specimens, now thoroughly established, will maintain their annual rate of quick growth until they have matured, when the rate will drop.

Some of the best-loved native plants are reputedly difficult to propagate. Among these is the Trailing Arbutus (*Epigaea repens*), which, however, gave almost 100 per cent rooting from cuttings inserted during July in two successive years. Equally good results are obtained from shoots of the current season and those which were cut to include an inch or two of wood of the preceding season.

A flat is filled with a 50-50 mixture of sand and peat moss. A slit trench is made by pressing in a ruler. The cutting in the foreground is of the current season's growth, the one to the rear has about 1 inch of the wood of the preceding year.

The cuttings are inserted more or less horizontally with the objective of having the underside of the leaves as close as possible to the rooting medium.

When all cuttings were inserted, the soil surface was covered with a layer of Sphagnum Moss. Whether or not there is any special advantage in this I am unable to say. It did seem, though, that in the one row which was left uncovered the roots were not quite so heavily produced as in the moss-covered section.

The flat was then covered with a pane of glass to increase the humidity in the vicinity of the cuttings and to reduce the need for watering. The glass covering was tilted about 1 inch with the lower edge ideally falling ½ inch short of the side wall of the flat; thus rain falling on the glass ran down into the rooting medium, through which it was dispersed by capillarity. This was done to avoid as far as possible the use of our well water, which is alkaline—pH 7.5.

The following spring the cuttings were well rooted and the most difficult part of the operation is to be done—that of transplanting them without too much loss.

One fairly certain method to avoid any root disturbance whatever is by planting the cuttings in a container, buried so that the rim is a little bit below the surrounding soil. If this is not convenient or if you want plants to give away to friends, they can be potted in 3½-inch pots, which preferably should be kept in a shaded and partly closed cold frame for a few weeks.

Wintertime cuttings

Many plants, especially the narrow-leaved evergreens, can be rooted from cuttings which are made during October, November, and December.

There are two methods of making cuttings of Arborvitae. One is to cut off a small branch with a sharp knife.

Another is to pull off a small branch—this is known as taking a cutting with a heel.

Here are samples of various cone-bearing evergreens to indicate the size of cuttings preferred—the labels are 6 inches long. There are two types of cuttings, the left one of each pair is made with a heel.

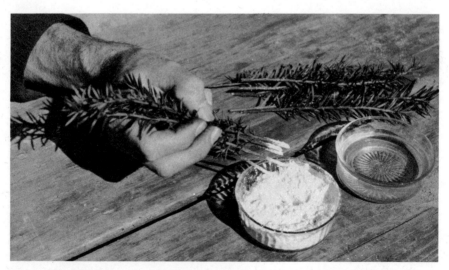

Often the use of a root-inducing growth regulator such as Hormodin or Rootone is helpful. The method of application is to take a half-dozen or so prepared cuttings, dip the butts in a saucer of water, shake off the surplus, and then dip them into a container of the root-inducing powder.

A flat filled with sand, the cuttings closely inserted in rows, and made firm by tamping the sand.

Cuttings are given a thorough soaking to help settle further the sand and the flat is then put in a cold frame and left there all winter. In order to protect them from severe freezing they can be given a light sprinkle of excelsior or salt-marsh hay. The sash is put on and during severe weather it is covered with an old quilt or a layer of salt-marsh hay. If it is not convenient to put them in a cold frame, they could be put, as these were, on a glass-enclosed, unheated porch until late in November, when there was danger of their freezing. They were then brought into my study and placed on the floor and kept there until April, when they were taken back to the porch.

A homemade propagating case. This may be a box, 12 by 9 by 5 inches, with a transparent superstructure which consists of two pieces of glass 12 inches wide by 10 inches high for the sides and two pieces 8¾ inches wide by 10 inches high to form the ends. These are put in place before the rooting medium, which helps to hold them upright. The corners at the top can be fastened together with strips of Scotch Tape. The roof is a piece of glass 13 by 9½ inches which rests on the side walls. This propagating case was kept all winter in the bay window of my study. This was a little too warm for best results, even though the temperature dropped at times to 45°. Ideally they should be placed in a cold greenhouse where the temperature is maintained between 45 and 50°.

Here are samples taken on May 26 showing the roots produced in vermiculite. These, except for the Juniper at the left, are ready either to be potted or to be "lined out."

A similar lot taken from the flat of sand. Although roots of these are not so far advanced as those above, they ultimately came along and about 80 per cent rooted.

Hardwood cuttings of deciduous shrubs

Many deciduous shrubs can be propagated by means of hardwood cuttings which are taken any time during the winter, but preferably as early as possible after the leaves are fallen.

Cuttings are made of shoots which grew during the preceding growing season. Some of them are satisfactory only when the cutting contains a terminal bud, including Rose-of-Sharon (*Hibiscus syriacus*) and Weigela. With the majority of the shrubs suitable for propagation in this way the entire length of the shoot can be used, cutting it into pieces 6 to 10 inches long, preferably with at least three nodes, or "joints." When cuttings are made in this way, it is important that the proximal ends should point in the same direction. They are then tied into bundles and are either buried in a sandy knoll where the drainage is perfect or are put into layers in boxes and covered with moist sand, peat moss, or sawdust. Ideally they should be exposed to a temperature of 65° or 70° for four or five weeks to initiate the formation of callus, after which the temperature should be lowered to 35° to 40°. Your choice of either of these two methods you use depends on whether you have suitable storage space, such as a garage or unheated cellar where the low temperatures prevail.

In the spring the cuttings should be planted outdoors, with only the terminal bud showing above the surface, set about 6 inches apart in rows 2 feet apart.

Cuttings are made in lengths of from 6 to 10 inches, preferably with at least three nodes. They can be cut with either a knife or pruning shears, making the cut a quarter to a half inch below the joint.

Those species which root easily may be cut with sharp shears. With more difficult ones it is better to use a sharp knife.

When the cuttings are made, they are tied into bundles of twenty-five or less, each one labeled with the name of the plant. With the butts of the cuttings all pointing in the same direction the cuttings are then covered with moist sand or peat moss or sawdust and kept in a cold cellar during the winter. The temperature should be from 65° to 70° for four or five weeks, then it should be reduced to 40°.

A bundle of Weigela cuttings removed from sand storage. Note the callus especially on the center cutting. There is too much top growth at this stage for best results.

Cuttings in water

This is a favorite method of many amateurs. Personally I don't particularly care for it because the roots tend to clump together when they are removed from the water and it is difficult to spread them naturally when potting them. It can be done however by following the method described on page 93.

Boxwood (*Buxus sempervirens rotundifolia*). At the left are new shoots put in during July 1953; only one rooted. At the right are cuttings of older wood made in April of the same year, three of nine well rooted, four starting, two no signs of roots. They were kept on the shelf in my study, where they stood still until the summer of 1954. Photographed August 17, 1954. Obviously this is not a good method in this particular case.

Cuttings of the Golden Weeping Willow. These are nearly ready for planting outdoors; larger cuttings could have been used.

Growth made by Dwarf Arctic Willow (*Salix purpurea nana*), from cuttings started in water in the spring. Photograph was made in the early fall of the same year.

Shows the excellent root system.

Cutting of Michaelmas Daisy, or Hardy Aster (*Aster novi-belgi*), which took to the water. The propagation of Hardy Asters in this way is a possible means of by-passing a wilt disease that affects them.

Cutting of Oleander: A few pieces of charcoal to absorb obnoxious gasses are recommended by garden writers, but I doubt very much if it has much effect on rooting one way or the other.

Cuttings of Saintpaulia (African-violet) rooted in water. (See also page 93.)

Leaf cuttings

Leaf cuttings offer the gardener a ready means whereby some plants can be propagated. Ordinarily the plants originated this way are replicas of the parents, but, as noted below, there are some exceptions.

There are numerous plants which are viviparous (producing buds which are capable of regeneration), such as Pickaback-plant (*Tolmiea Menziesi*) and some varieties of Water-lily which produce plantlets on the leaves. Another example is the plant variously known as Sprouting-leaf, Miracle-leaf, Air-plant, Life-plant, Good-luck-leaf, and Floppers.

Pickaback-plant—when growing in the wild, the outer leaves of the Pickaback-plant ultimately topple over to the ground, where the plantlets on the leaves take root and grow. In propagating them under artificial conditions they can be cut off with 1½-inch leafstalks and dibbled into individual flowerpots in the standard 1-1-1 mixture. Keep them shaded for a few weeks.

Many tropical Water-lilies have viviparous leaves. The one shown here is Dauben Water-lily (*Nymphaea Daubeniana*). Notice the plantlets that surround the main plant. Before cold weather comes in the fall, these leaves may be cut off and each one put in a water-holding container at least 4 inches deep and 1 foot or more across. This should be filled with soil to within 1 inch of the top, in which the plantlet is placed. Then the container should be filled to the brim with water. Keep it in a sunny window or in a greenhouse with a minimum temperature of about 60° until it has warmed up enough out-doors to warrant placing it out, usually about the first week in June in the vicinity of New York City. If more than one or two plants are needed, a tank of some kind is necessary. In this case the plantlets should be potted in 4-inch pots which are submerged about 3 inches below the surface of the water.

Kalanchoë (Bryophyllum) pinnata produces plantlets in the notches along the leaf margins. These in nature or in the greenhouse fall off and, if the environment is suitable, they quickly grow.

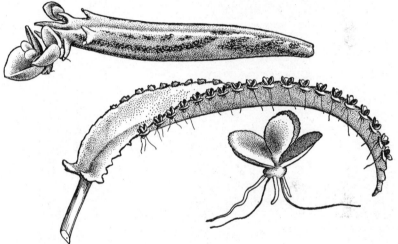

K. Daigremontiana and *K. verticillata* behave similarly, except that the plantlets develop only at the leaf tips on the latter.

Sedum Morganianum (Donkey's Tail) and others also propagate themselves in the same way.

Adult plant of Donkey's Tail.

Almost any of the subtropical species of Sedum, Echeveria, etc., can be propagated by pulling off leaves and sticking their bases in a flat of the 1-1-1 mixture. *Echeveria Weinbergi,* leaf cuttings in the foreground.

Sedum species with leaf cuttings at right.

Peperomia obtusifolia, with leaf cuttings in various stages.

Pot containing leaf cuttings of Saintpaulia (African-violet). These were inserted on May 18, photographed October 25 the same year. The precocious one in bloom is Sir Launcelot (My daughter wants to know "Where is Fair Elaine?").

Rooted plants, more than one per leaf. The original leaf can be replanted if you want more plants. These usually look like the parent, but occasionally a single leaf may go haywire and produce plants that bear either pink, white, or purple flowers, or produce different kinds of leaves. These are known as mutations.

A leaf cutting of Saintpaulia rooted in water. This method is preferable to the one frequently recommended of covering a jar with waxed paper in which holes are punched, through which the leaf stalks are pushed into the water. The leaf also benefits from the extra humidity conferred by the partial enclosure.

A leaf of *Begonia Rex* is cut with 1-inch leafstalk (petiole) and the main veins severed. The stalk is inserted in the sand so that the entire leaf lies flat on the rooting medium. It may be necessary to put two or three stones on the leaf to hold it down, or, if you have any hairpins, you can pin it down with them.

If preferred, the leaf can be cut to wedge-shaped pieces, each containing a main vein.

Leaf-bud cuttings

Toward the close of the 1920's, Dr. Henry T. Skinner, now director of the National Arboretum, worked on leaf-bud cuttings of Rhododendrons and obtained excellent results. The cuttings were made late in July and were inserted in a mixture of three parts, by bulk, of New Jersey quartz sand and two parts of peat moss. They were treated with a growth regulator (root-inducing

Snake-plant (*Sansevieria trifasciata Laurenti*)—leaves cut into pieces 3 to 6 inches long root readily, but the characteristic yellow stripes of *Laurenti* are lacking in the progeny.

chemical, indolebutyric acid). The cuttings were placed in a propagating frame in a greenhouse. After rooting they were put on a greenhouse bench and kept at 75° to 80° to induce the basal buds to start into growth. They can be kept growing by maintaining them in a warm temperature, but it probably would be better to harden them off gradually and keep them cool (40°) during the winter. The varietal response varies considerably. It would happen that the only Rhododendrons I had available, *R. carolinianum* and *R. maximum*, were of the difficult, cantankerous kinds.

Leaf-bud cutting of *Rhododendron decorum*.

Left, root development of *R. decorum* a few weeks later. Right, root ball and shoot about five months after cutting was made.

Branch of Rhododendron showing kind of shoots from which buds may be cut.

Leaf-bud cuttings of *R. maximum*.

Cuttings made and inserted in flat with constant mist.

Root cuttings

One advantage to be gained from increasing plants by root cuttings is that little is needed in the way of skill or equipment to be successful. Grafted varieties, of course, should not be propagated by root cuttings because the understock is different from the top and, for garden purposes, usually inferior. But for others that are amenable (see lists below) it is an effective way of propagation.

In the fall dig up the roots of the variety selected for propagation. If it is herbaceous and a number of new plants are desired, the entire plant may be dug up to supply a sufficient number of roots. If, however, only a few new plants are needed, enough roots can be obtained by pushing in a spade alongside the clump and prying outward. In the case of trees and shrubs the best method is usually to dig into the soil about midway between the outermost spread of the branches and the center of the bush or tree to get the fairly young, vigorous roots. Be very sure that the roots you dig up belong to the plant you wish to propagate!

The thickness of the desirable roots varies according to the species. With Phlox, for example, the stringlike roots—about ⅒ inch in diameter—not the whiskery ones—are suitable; those of Japanese Anemone are ⅛ inch or a little larger; while in the case of woody plants they may be up to ½ inch across.

Before insertion the roots are cut into lengths of about 2 to 6 inches and are equally spaced in rows about 2 inches apart on the surface of the rooting medium made up of a mixture of sand, soil, and peat moss in equal parts, placed in a flat, and pressed down fairly firmly to 1 inch below the rim. They are then covered with ½ to 1 inch of sand and watered thoroughly. When only a few plants are required, several kinds can be put in labeled rows in each flat. During winter the flats are kept in a cold frame and after a few frosts are mulched with light, littery material such as Oak leaves or excelsior and left until spring.

In the spring shoots will appear above ground and, when they have attained a height of about 3 inches, the plantlets may be transplanted to a nursery row or other convenient place outdoors and shaded for a few weeks. Some of the late-flowering herbaceous plants may give a few blooms the first season if growing conditions are good, but don't expect them to be at their best until the following year.

Among woody plants these are listed as capable of propagation by root cuttings:

Aesculus parviflora (Bottlebrush Buckeye)
Albizzia Julibrissin ("Mimosa")
Calycanthus (Sweet-shrub)
Campsis (Trumpet-creeper)
Catalpa (Indian-bean)
Celastrus (Bittersweet)
Cladrastis (Yellow-wood)
Clerodendron (Glory Bower)
Halesia (Silver Bell)
Hypericum (St.-Johns-Wort)
Ilex (Holly)
Koelreuteria (Goldenrain-tree)
Maclura (Osage-orange)
Paulownia (Empress Tree)
Rhus (Sumac, Smoke-tree)
Robinia (Rose-acacia, Clammy Locust)
Sassafras
Stephanandra
Wisteria.

Some writers claim that Lilac can be propagated by root cuttings. I have been successful in rooting pieces of the underground parts of Lilac suckers, but pieces of true root always failed.

Herbaceous plants that can be propagated by root cuttings include:

Acanthus
Anchusa (Alkanet)
Anemone japonica, A. hupehensis (probably a form of *A. japonica*)
Bocconia (Plume-poppy)
Dicentra (Bleeding-heart)
Echinops (Globe-thistle)
Gypsophila (Babys-breath)*

* *Not the double-flowered kinds when they are grafted on* G. paniculata.

Morisia
Oenothera (Evening-primrose)
Papaver (Oriental Poppy)
Phlox (Garden Phlox)
Primula
Stokesia (Stokes-aster)
Trollius (Globe-flower)
Verbascum (Mullein)

Although the plants originated from root cuttings normally produce plants exactly the same as the parent, there are a few exceptions, notably in the case of Bouvardia variety Bridesmaid, and some of the fancy-leaved Pelargoniums (House Geranium).

Digging for roots of *Anemone japonica*. A deer chewed up most of the parent plant in the background.

The roots are laid out on a patch of sand so that they are more readily seen.

They are being cut up into pieces about 1 to 2 inches long and placed in a flat prepared as suggested in the introduction.

Kept in a cold frame over winter, they look like this the following May. One plant in the foreground, left, has been dug up to show the new roots.

A one-year-old Phlox plant, which grew from a piece of root similar to those shown left of the black pencil. The piece of root from which this plant grew is contained between the points of the two pencils.

Cuttings of herbaceous perennials

These can be made at various seasons, depending on the kinds. For example, Chrysanthemum and Hardy Aster, which bloom late in the year, can be propagated by cuttings made in early spring, when the young shoots are starting out from the rootstock. Delphinium cuttings may be taken in the spring and also in the summer when new shoots start from the ground line. With all the above it is desirable to make the cuts just below the surface when the shoots are from 3 to 6 inches long. When Chrysanthemums are required in quantity, the tips of rooted cuttings may be used as cuttings when they are 8 to 10 inches tall by removing the top third.

Gypsophila can be rooted if shoots are taken in early spring before the flower buds are formed. Viola cuttings can be made in July or August, *Alyssum saxatile,* Arabis, and Dianthus whenever the new growth is at the right stage—usually just after the flowers have faded.

Chrysanthemum cuttings in foreground taken from a stock plant, February 2, are being inserted in a 1-1-1 mixture, surfaced with sand. Notice the method of making the rooting medium firm at the base of the cutting.

Cuttings on March 15 are well rooted and ready to be potted.

A slightly richer soil mixture, which can be made by omitting the sand from the 1-1-1 mixture, is desirable when they are potted individually in 3-inch pots.

Now for a few odds and ends: Wounding the part of the cutting that is to be below ground in many cases is effective in helping to root difficult species. The wounds can be made by cutting a vertical slit with a sharp knife or by cutting off a slice of bark and wood.

Growth regulators or root-inducing hormones have a place in plant propagation. Though they cannot replace the regular care of the cuttings, they usually can be relied on to induce the cuttings to root earlier and to produce roots in greater numbers. They are obtainable under various trade names. Those containing indole-butyric acid seem to be preferred. No matter which kind you use, be sure to follow the manufacturer's directions as given on the label.

Abrasives, because of their irritant effect, are used sometimes as rooting media. Powdered pumice and powdered glass are said to be used effectively in rooting difficult alpines. The pumice is mixed in the proportion of five parts to two parts sand; powdered glass, three parts to one of sand. You can probably get the pumice from a hardware store—ask for their coarsest grade; the glass might be obtained from a sandpaper manufacturer, or you can make your own by putting glass in a bottomless box on a concrete floor and pounding it with a road rammer.

Those who are interested in the kinks and quirks attendant on the rooting of cuttings should look over the Propagation Notebook in the Appendix. The cuttings were inserted in a cold frame as described above.

NEW AND UNUSUAL METHODS

Polythene

During the past three or four years polythene, a plastic film, has been used as an aid in rooting cuttings and as a covering for the rooting medium in air-layering. This material has the faculty of permitting the passage of air and to a large extent preventing transmission of water vapor. Polythene is available under various trade names such as Polyethylene, Alathon, Tralon, Pearlon, Dura-clear, etc. Polythene films are available in various thicknesses ranging from 1/1000 of an inch to 8/1000. According to Donald Wyman in the *Arnold Arboretum Garden Book*, the amount of water vapor transmitted during twenty-four hours ranges from 0.95 to 0.15. This represents the number of grams lost per 100 square inches of exposed film surface during twenty-four hours. A comparatively thick film is probably better to use for rooting cuttings. The method is to insert the cuttings at the right time for each species. Then the cuttings are covered with the plastic, put on in such a way that there are no openings of any kind. The following picures show the technique I used.

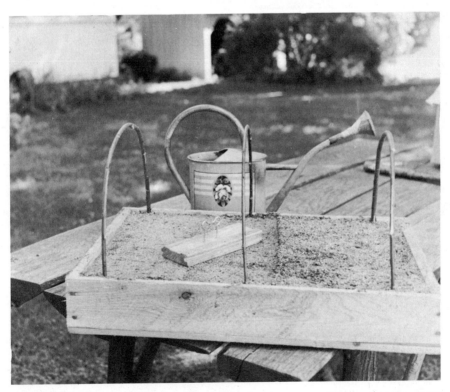

A flat is filled with a mixture of sand and peat moss—75 per cent sand, 25 per cent peat moss by bulk. A tamper, in this case consisting of a section of flooring with two screw hooks, which serve as a handle, is used to firm the rooting medium. The left half has been pressed down so that the surface is ½ inch below the rim of the flat.

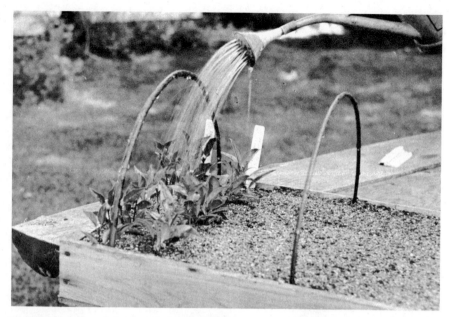

It is important to prevent wilting of cuttings. To this end the work is done in the shade, and whenever a row is finished, it is watered in thoroughly.

The method of inserting cuttings with the aid of a dibble. A hole is made, the cutting put in with its base touching the bottom of the hole, and the rooting medium is firmed by pushing the soil around the base with a dibble as shown (August 14).

Another method is to make a slit in the rooting medium. The tamper serves as a guide for the kitchen knife which is used to make the slit. The cuttings are inserted and the soil is firmed from the side.

The Covered Wagon! The flat has been filled with cuttings and plastic is applied and tacked down. The half hoops are made from flexible stems of weeping willow which were treated to prevent them from growing by heating them over an electric burner.

In this picture representative samples of each kind of cutting were removed on September 24. Only one (*Cytisus praecox*—Early Broom) had formed roots.

So the plastic was reapplied and the flat was put in a cold frame with the hope that the unrooted cuttings would come through the winter and perhaps start a new growth the following year.

As soon as the cuttings were placed, vermiculite was poured in around to help avoid violent fluctuations of temperature. It will be noticed that the potted plants, in foreground and at right, also were covered.

The flat of cuttings as it appeared the following spring. The results were disappointing. The Cytisus had rooted 100 per cent; the remainder varied, some being dead and the others in no case had more than about 10 per cent rooted.

This method was not entirely successful in this particular case. Probably poor results can be attributed to the fact that cuttings of some species were not inserted early enough in the season and the covering was not tight enough to retain moisture.

It is interesting that *Cytisus praecox* is the only species that rooted 100 per cent. This surprised me because I had looked on this as being difficult to root, especially when two-year-old shoots were used. In my previous experience with this plant it was the current season's shoots only which were successful.

Polythene is a versatile material. In addition to the use cited above it can serve as a cover for grafted scions in top-worked trees; and, cut into narrow strips, it can be used to tie in buds.

Constant mist

During the past three or four years considerable interest has developed in what is called a "fog box," or "constant mist," method for rooting cuttings. My experience with it during the last two years has been of absorbing interest. Essentially the method is one of rooting cuttings in the open in full sun, preventing them from wilting by keeping the foliage constantly moist by means of nozzles which deliver water in a fine mist. Later developments seem to indicate that intermittent mist may be preferable from the standpoint of the welfare of the plants and because it uses less water and thus is more economical.

For my first setup I contrived an enclosure made of plastic film attached to builder's laths. The reason for making this corral was that a windy spot was the only convenient place to install it; and it seemed to me that it would help to confine the fog and prevent it from being blown away from the plants. Even though it is considered unnecessary to keep the mist going during the hours of darkness, the mist was left on day and night from early June until frost. The second year the corral was dispensed with and a smaller nozzle was installed, which seemed to work as well or even better than the enclosed system. Apparently there is enough variation in the direction and force of the air currents so that almost invariably no part of the area, ordinarily covered by the spray, was without moisture long enough to injure the cuttings.

My good friend Sven Sward, horticulturist at Vassar College, after he saw my first setup devised a similar but smaller box which was installed in a greenhouse. He had no difficulty in rooting a variety of plants. (See page 147.)

Guy wires at each corner of the enclosure were fastened to heavy stakes to anchor it.

This shows the enclosure which was devised to serve as a windbreak for a "fog box." It was made by tacking polythene plastic onto 4-foot building laths. Two sides were removable. The purpose of the grating, of pine 1 by 1 inch, is to eliminate any danger of the rooting material becoming waterlogged. The fog came from the nozzle attached to a piece of flexible copper tubing, which in turn was attached to a hose connected with the domestic water supply.

The boxes are about 1 foot square and 6 inches deep; 4 inches would be better because half a cubic foot of sand is too heavy for convenient handling. A strip of metal fly screening is put over crack in the box to prevent the rooting medium from sifting through.

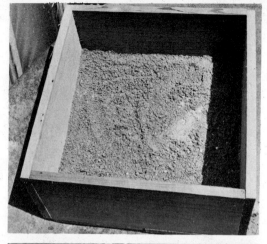

A 2-inch layer of coarse sand is put in to ensure adequate drainage.

Two broom clamps were used to hold the removable side in place.

Humidification without windbreak. The Arrow points to the nozzle. This is a Bete fog nozzle, C. series, which gave perfect performance in making a very fine mist without any clogging. It was a great improvement over the preceding year, when nozzles of a different make were constantly clogging.

A similar fog box on a smaller scale set up at Vassar College under greenhouse conditions.

This is a commercial use of the constant-mist system, in a deep cold frame.

Another commercial use of the constant-mist system, in a greenhouse.

A novel application of constant mist is shown here. Fred Heutte, superintendent of parks, Norfolk, Va., provided the following information. The scions were inserted on a cut-back Camellia on July 15. They were kept under mist from 7 A.M. until 6 P.M. every day except rainy ones. On September 15 the union was good enough to warrant discontinuing the mist. The following February 23 they were in good shape except for tip burn of the immature growth.

Cuttings of *Daphne Cneorum* (Rose Daphne) from vermiculite—50 per cent rooted.

From peat and sand—90 per cent rooted.

From sand—100 per cent rooted. It is interesting to notice that the larger cuttings containing two-year-old wood as well as that of the current season rooted as well as, or better than, the new wood. All of the above were inserted on June 19; they were rooted by the middle of July.

At the end of July it was decided to move these plants from the fog box. Accordingly a flat was prepared by putting an inch or so of partly decayed leaves in the bottom, which was surfaced with 2½ inches of sifted 1-1-1 mixture. (See Chapter IX.)

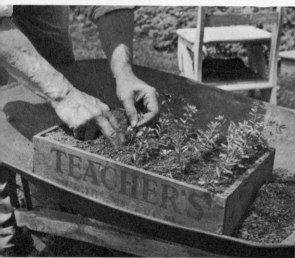

This picture shows a technique of planting rooted cuttings. The soil is not at first packed down, which allows the holes to be made easily with the fingers, to receive the roots. Firming is done after the roots are in place.

One of the advantages of the constant mist is that cuttings larger than would normally be used often root with greater ease than the orthodox smaller cuttings. Here are cuttings of Meyer's Lilac (*Syringa Meyeri*). Note the good root system developed on three of the larger cuttings.

Two of these were potted immediately. They were returned to the fog box for a week or two, then plunged into soil in partial shade.

One interesting thing about this system of plant propagation is that some cuttings make an excessively large callus. Varieties even within the species are more prone to this than others. A plant propagator does not like to see excessively large calluses because apparently roots are seldom formed when these conditions occur. Among the treatments recommended are: dipping the callus in a rooting powder (left) and paring off excess callus growth (right).

Here are the results. The two cuttings on the left show still more callus growth as a result of the powder treatment. Three in the middle are those that were pared and those at the right, one of which produced roots, received no treatment.

Cuttings of *Rhododendron Kaempferi*.

Cuttings of *Cytisus praecox*. Notice that it is the largest cutting that has the most roots.

After two or three frosts the rooted cuttings, including those which had been potted up, were packed as closely as possible in the corral.

Salt marsh hay was packed between the walls and the flats. A
thin covering was put over the
plants.

The two removable sides were
loosened at the top and brought
together to make a sort of peaked
roof.

The results when cuttings are subjected to constant mist were
astounding. Large cuttings, in general, rooted better than the
small cuttings of current-year wood, which used to be considered
essential. Plants that were thought to be somewhat difficult—
Daphne, Cytisus, and the Star Magnolia—rooted with ease. Cuttings of purple Lilac rooted 100 per cent, while those of a white
Lilac (shown on page 151) only one of seven rooted.

It has been suggested that constant mist is better adapted to southern regions than to the northern. This is supported to some extent by Sven Sward's success in carrying over winter in a cool greenhouse the following plants: American Holly (*Ilex opaca*), Dogwood (pink-flowering), Leucothoë, *Picea excelsa nana, Metasequoia glyptostroides, Pieris japonica,* Retinispora, Rhododendron, *Viburnum Sieboldi.* These were potted in September and planted out in a cold frame the following March. During the following winter they were protected by covering them with leaves and glass sash. Mr. Sward reports that about 70 per cent of the plants rooted; rather surprisingly Hemlock was a complete failure.

Early Broom (*Cytisus praecox*) and Lavender are xerophytes—that is, plants that are adapted to growing under very dry conditions. Surprisingly they reveled in the humidity. One might expect that fungus diseases would be rife under constant mist, but such is not the case. Neither mildew nor black spot put in an appearance.

My cuttings looked hoary because of the deposit of lime from the hard water that comes from our well; in the Pleasant Acres Nurseries at Newburgh, N.Y., the cuttings were a brownish color derived from the peat-bog water that was used.

The chief objection I have to this system is the difficulty of carrying the rooted cuttings over the winter, and I am not alone in this. A friend who rooted hundreds of cuttings of *Magnolia stellata* with 100 per cent "take" reported that he lost half of them when they were transplanted the following spring.

There are still some "bugs" in the method which I expect will be ironed out by being careful to harden the cuttings off by gradually increasing the length of the periods during which the water is shut off. Also it may be desirable to start the cuttings at the earliest practicable date, so that they can be potted up in time for them to make additional roots before the winter sets in.

CHAPTER IV

Bulbs, corms, tubers, rhizomes, rootstocks

COMMERCIAL growers in their catalogues often lump all these together under "bulbs," which makes some pernickety botanists gnash their teeth. This is how they differ:

Bulbs are made up of closely packed, fleshy scale leaves attached to a comparatively small basal plate of solid tissue; examples are Tulip, Narcissus, and Lily.

Corms are similar in appearance to bulbs, differing in being solid throughout with small buds ultimately forming on the top; examples are Gladiolus and Crocus.

Corm of Gladiolus at left; bulb of Narcissus at right.

Cutaway view of Tulip bulb, showing tiny blossom and closely packed leaves attached to basal plate.

Tubers may be swollen roots, as in the Dahlia, Begonia, and Cyclamen, or swollen stems, as in the case of the Jerusalem Artichoke and the Potato.

A *rhizome* is a thickened shoot that grows underground or along the soil surface, producing roots from its undersides and leaves or shoots above the ground; examples are the Bearded Iris and Solomons Seal. When these shoots are short and stubby, as in Canna, they are named *rootstock*. Trillium, according to *Gray's Manual,* is a "praemorse tuber-like rootstock."

Bulbs, corms, tubers, rhizomes, and rootstocks are storage organs full of food which enable the species to survive unfavorable climates. *Bulbils* are the little bulbs that form on the aerial stems of Lilies and other plants; *bulblets* are those that form underground.

These specialized structures in most cases afford us ready means of propagation (the exception being Cyclamen), because at some time in their growth cycles they are more nearly dormant than plants without these structures and can be manipulated without much injury.

Bulbs

Many bulbs propagate themselves naturally by breaking up into a number of small bulbs. Tulips do this especially when they are planted shallowly. In the case of Daffodils the mother bulb makes offsets which are known as "slabs."

The Hyacinth is a shy propagator under natural conditions, but by processing a dormant bulb it is possible to increase greatly the number of bulblets. There are two methods commonly used—"scooping" and "scoring." The first named results in a greater production of bulblets, but usually they are slightly smaller than those produced by scoring. A potato- or melon-baller is an ideal tool for scooping. If you do not have ready access to such a tool, you may file a teaspoon to make a sharp edge and use it instead. Don't sacrifice your best silver—buy a stainless-steel one from a five-and-dime store.

This picture shows the beginning of the removal of the basal plate to expose the scale leaves which make up a large portion of the bulb.

The job is completed.

In scoring, three cuts are made in the base, extending about a third of the way into the bulb.

The bulbs are placed upside-down in a temperature of about 70° or 80°. After a lapse of two or three months they looked like these, which should be planted in the fall, still upside-down, covered with two or three inches of soil.

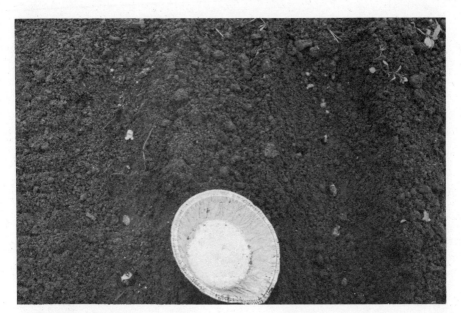

The following year they are dug up, when the foliage has withered, and separated. They are then planted about 3 inches apart in rows 1 foot apart, to grow into bulbs of flowering size, which may take from three to six years.

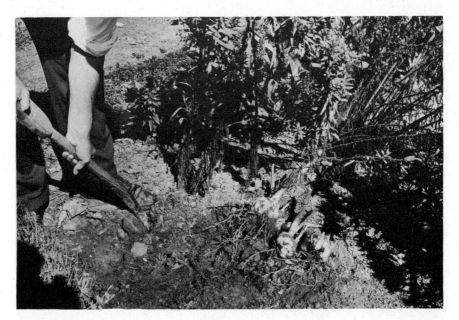

When Lilies have been growing in one spot for a number of years, the bulbs are likely to become too crowded for best results. The ideal time to divide them is when the foliage is becoming yellow.

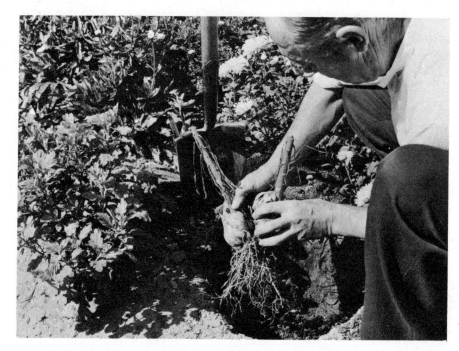

Here is a "double" bulb of the Madonna Lily being pulled apart. Do not cut off the roots.

The bulbs are reset from 6 to 8 inches apart. Madonna Lilies are planted so that there are no more than 2 inches of soil covering them. Most Lilies, however, require deeper planting than this.

Another method is to pull up the Lily stems and heel them in as soon as the flowers show signs of wilting.

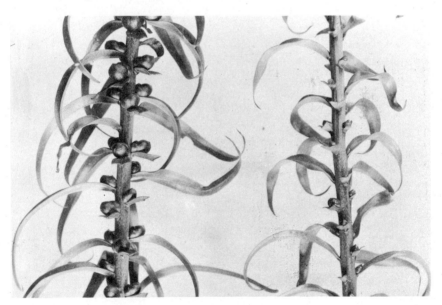

Many kinds of Lilies propagate by means of stem bulbils—*Lilium sulphureum,* for example. There are at least two ways by which the number and size of bulbils can be increased. One is by removal of the flowers in the bud stage, as was done with the one at the left.

This may result in numerous bulblets such as these (*Lilium hollandicum*).

Lilium candidum at left; *Lilium umbellatum* at right. The two growing points on *Lilium candidum* indicate that the following year there will be at least two flower stalks from this bulb. Notice the bulblets on the underground part of the stem of *Lilium umbellatum*.

The plant of *Lilium umbellatum* denuded of the bulblets which have been planted separately. Also a dozen or more of the outer scale leaves have been removed for propagation. About one half of them were completely buried ½ inch deep in the flat. Those remaining were planted with the tips showing above the surface.

Two months later.

Bulblets produced from scales of *Lilium leucanthum.*

Corms

Recently dug specimens of Gladiolus, showing new corms produced on top of the old ones that were planted in May.

Four new corms plus four cormels were produced from the corm in the center of the cluster. The corms are of flowering size. The cormels will take a year at least before reaching flowering size. Ordinarily many more cormels are produced. These can be planted in the spring in rows in the same way as you would plant peas.

Tubers

Tuber of *Gloriosa Rothschildiana*. The growing tip is at the left.

Planting in a 6-inch pot. This one had to be put in diagonally because it was too big to be placed upright.

The increase by the end of the growing season. The old tuber is in the middle with two new ones, right and left. Division of the tubers is another way of increasing one's stock of Gloriosa.

Tuberous Begonias can be multiplied by dividing the tubers. It is necessary or at least desirable to wait until new growth has started before any cutting is done.

Shows the method of making the cut when two shoots are growing close together.

It is advisable to treat the cut surface with a fungicide. Here a mixture of 10 per cent fermate and 90 per cent dusting sulphur is being used. The applicator consists of a tuft of lamb's wool fastened to the end of a straightened-out paper clip.

Tuberous Begonias can also be propagated from stem cuttings.

These can be rooted in a standard 1-1-1 mixture with which a 3- or 4-inch pot is filled without packing it down. The hole to receive the cutting can be made by pushing the finger in the center. The cutting is then put in with its base resting on the bottom of the hole and the soil is firmed by pressing it down with thumbs or fingers.

The leaf surface can be reduced by cutting off a portion of one of the leaves.

The cutting is then put in a plastic bag (see page 87) to maintain moist atmosphere, which prevents it from wilting. It is advisable to keep the cutting in the shade until it is well rooted.

Inserted during July, by September the cutting (right) had rooted and made enough new growth to blossom.

Dahlias can be propagated by division of the rootstock. It is essential to have a portion of the stem attached to the root.

Tuberous rooted Begonias can be propagated from seeds, which must be sown indoors in January or February to be sure of getting flowers from them the same year. Follow the procedure for small seeds (see pages 28–33). Named varieties or any specially good ones you may have raised from seeds can be propagated by cutting the tubers and by making stem cuttings as described above.

Rhizomes

The most familiar of rhizomatous plants are the Tall Bearded Irises. They can be increased in short order by dividing the rhizomes between July and October.

A clump is dug up and the old flower stalks are cut off close to the rhizome.

The leaves are cut back to within a third of their length. They are now ready for planting in a hole with a ridge of soil on which the rhizome is placed, with the roots spread out on either side. (This division is capable of being further divided to make two plants.)

The roots have been covered with earth which is firmed by standing on it.

Rootstocks

Among the native plants that might be considered difficult to propagate either sexually by seeds or asexually by division of the rootstock is the Trillium. The pictures which follow, taken by Walter E. Thwing, formerly publisher of *Home Garden*, show how, by surgery, it is possible to hurry up nature.

Washing away the soil of a potted plant to expose the crown of the rootstock, without disturbing the roots, reveals the growing bud of next year's plant already well along in July. A notch is cut just below the bud at the point indicated by the knife. The plant is then re-covered with soil and the pot plunged in a shady spot.

In October, three months after the notching, results are plain. The large bud is the one shown above. Three strong new shoots have broken out just below the notch, and there is evidence of more coming. The only reason for uncovering the plant at this stage was to get this picture.

The first spring after the surgical treatment seven plants appeared instead of the two whose stems are shown in illustration. Four of them bore large flowers, although only two are visible here. The pot was posed to enable you to count the stems rather than to display the blossoms.

In July of the second year our busy clump, uncovered just to satisfy curiosity, showed several little new rootstocks and many more buds.

In October the whole clump was removed from the pot for separation. Five new rootstocks were strong enough to start alone.

The five new rootstocks have been cut from the mother plant and are ready to be potted up alone. (The white disc under each is a pinhead.) Original rootstock continues to make new offsets.

The second spring the five new rootstocks produced eight. The original root-stock produced six, of which four have flowers despite division made the previous fall.

The photograph shows dividends paid in less than three years. The new rootstocks produced nine plants, eight of them with blossoms. The original rootstock increased to sixteen and now is ready for further division.

And now Mr. Thwing tells us how *not* to propagate a Trillium. Complete decapitation of the rootstock proved to be fatal.

The vertical cuttings of the rootstock, although they had strong-looking roots, failed to grow.

Horizontal cuttings of the rootstock also rotted away. The evidence of these unsuccessful methods of cutting, while perhaps not conclusive, suggests that they be avoided. The operations might have been successes, but the patients died.

CHAPTER V

Runners, offsets, stolons, and suckers

THE specialized shoots named above provide easy means of propagating the plants that bear them.

Runners are slender shoots which start, usually, near the base of the mother plant and produce roots and shoots at intervals. A well-known example is the Strawberry. Sometimes the flower stalks serve a similar purpose, as in the case of *Chlorophytum elatum*, sometimes called Spider-plant or Airplane-plant, and *Neomarica Northiana* (Apostle-plant).

An *offset* is similar but with a shorter stem, an example is Sempervivum.

A *stolon* is a shoot that starts above the surface of the ground and then bends over so that it comes in contact with the soil and forms roots. An example is *Cornus stolonifera* (Red-osier Dogwood). In some plants roots are formed only at the tip of the shoot, as in the case of Black Raspberry.

A *sucker* is a shoot that starts below the ground from a root or underground stem. Examples are Lilac and Red Raspberry.

Runners

Strawberry is commonly propagated by means of runners, which in most varieties are formed in great abundance during the growing season. Under home garden conditions these runners can be rooted in 3- or 4-inch pots, filled with rich soil, by pegging them down with a clothespin or something similar. The big advantage of this is that they can be planted without any setback in August, enabling them to produce a crop the following year.

Another runner-forming plant is the Creeping Bugle (*Ajuga reptans*). The small plants can be dug up at almost any season for increase, or they can be left in place to form a matted ground cover.

Some of the Bromeliads (relatives of the Pineapple) can be propagated by means of runners such as the one seen here, *Bromelia lasiantha*. These can be handled by removing the runner from the parent plant and putting it in as a cutting or can be rooted the same as Strawberry, by putting a soil-filled pot near the plant and waiting until it has formed roots before taking it away from the mother.

This is *Saxifraga sarmentosa*, a plant often called Strawberry-geranium or Strawberry-begonia. These common names are misnomers, because the plant is not Strawberry, Geranium, or Begonia. If you must have an English name for it, call it Mother-of-thousands. It is one of the easiest of all plants to propagate by taking the plantlets from the runners and putting them in separate flowerpots—3-inch size is ample to start them. (See also page 57.)

Spider-plant or Airplane-plant (*Chlorophytum elatum*) achieves the same effect by means of its flowering stems, which when the flowers have faded, produce numerous plantlets.

Offsets

Cobweb Houseleek (*Sempervivum arachnoideum*) is an example of a plant which makes offsets. These can be pulled off at any time except during winter, and dibbled in where they are to grow. The plants to the left, *Saxifraga aizoon* var. (Silver Saxifrage), with white-margined leaves, have offsets with even shorter stems. These need more care in handling than the Houseleeks. The entire plant should be dug up during the summer, the offsets pulled off and planted in individual 2½-inch pots, using a 1-1-1 soil mixture plus an added part of chicken grits—preferably limestone rather than granite. They should be kept in a cold frame, shaded and watered, with ample ventilation at all times until they are rooted.

Stolons

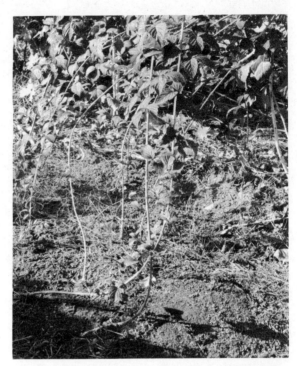

Black Raspberries propagate themselves by means of stolons, which in this picture may be seen arching over from the main plant in the background.

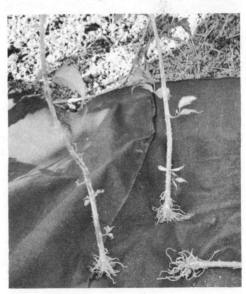

This is a closer view of the above.

Later the stolon develops a large root system suitable for planting.

Suckers

Suckers; Red Raspberries ordinarily are propagated by digging up suckers which appear alongside the main row. They can be dug up in the spring, cut back about one half, and transplanted.

CHAPTER VI

Layering

THIS is a means whereby plants which are difficult to root from cuttings can be propagated. There are three methods whereby this can be done—ground, mound, and air-layering. In ground-layering it is necessary that the plant to be propagated should have branches so disposed that they can be brought down to the ground and held there until sufficient roots are formed on the layers to permit them to be severed from the parent plants, for example as in the case of the Rhododendron pictured on pages 185–186.

Mound-layering is a commercial method used considerably in Europe, but in most cases it is only of academic interest to the amateur. Briefly, it involves cutting back a parent plant almost to the ground level in the spring. This causes abundant shoots to be produced suitable for this type of propagation. The following spring the parent plant is covered with a mound of earth. After a year or so the shoots make sufficient roots to enable them to be dug up and planted.

In air-layering a suitable shoot is selected, the stem is wounded by removal of a cylinder of bark, by cutting a notch, or by making a slit in the stem at the point where it is desired that roots should form. The old-fashioned way, suitable when done indoors, was to wrap the wound with a handful of Sphagnum Moss and cover it with waxed paper, tin foil, or some such waterproof covering, leaving the top open so that water can be applied to keep the moss moist as is shown on page 184. Recently, however, with the coming of the polythene plastic film, the moss is wetted to the right degree, put in place, covered tightly with the sheet of plastic, which has the faculty of keeping moisture in so that no watering is required until the rooted layer is severed from the parent plant. This method still has some "bugs" in it and I must admit that I, for one, have not had very much success with it. Apparently some failures can be attributed to the rooting medium's becoming too wet, either by rain or by exudation of water from the tree or shrub, or they may depend, to a large extent, on the kinds of plants to which the method is applied. The Arnold Arboretum experimented with a large number of different plants, some of which rooted 100 per cent while some failed completely. See the list in the Appendix.

Another hurdle which has to be overcome is that of caring for the rooted layers in such a way that they survive. This may involve potting the rooted layer and keeping it for a while in a closed cold frame and gradually inuring it to outdoor conditions by progressively admitting more air.

Ground layering

Soil is improved for ground-layering by mixing sand and peat moss in it.

The branch selected is shown held in the left hand of the operator.

A slit is cut in the stem at the point where roots are wanted.

The "tongue," made by cutting into the stem, is held open by a toothpick.

The wound is dusted with a root-inducing substance applied with a soft brush.

A trench 2 inches deep has been made and the shoot is held down by one hand. The other hand is being used to cover it with soil.

A sizable rock is then put over the layer and serves a double purpose of keeping the layer in place and of helping to conserve the moisture in the soil.

A year later the layer is ready to be transplanted. Notice the mass of roots, especially at the point where the root-inducing hormone was applied.

Air-layering

As may be seen by consulting the Appendix, air-layering is not always 100 per cent successful. One can learn from failures as well as by successes, so here is the sad story of my limited attempts to root plants with the aid of root-inducing hormones, Sphagnum Moss, and polythene wrapping.

Squeezing surplus moisture from the moss. About the right degree of moisture occurs when moss is saturated with water and then squeezed as hard as possible to remove the surplus.

A cylinder of bark is removed from a stem of Enkianthus.

The wound is dusted with a root-inducing hormone.

The moss is applied.

The plastic cover is held in place by tying tightly. (As it happened, this was not put on with sufficient care, and, owing to the smooth surface of the shoot on which the operation was performed, the covering worked down so that the treated area was for a few days exposed to sun and wind. Doubtless as a result of this the operation was unsuccessful.)

A notch is cut in a two-year-old shoot of Star Magnolia.

A root-inducing hormone is about to be applied, in this case the commercial preparation Air-wrap, in which a root-inducing hormone is combined with a polythene wrapper. In the left hand is a wad of moss. The plastic cover was then laid in place and tied tightly. This experiment was also unsuccessful, possibly because the layering was not started early enough in the spring.

An air layer of Dogwood.

At the close of the growing season the treated shoots were cut from the plant and the wrappings removed. While the wounded areas were callused, they were not rooted.

One of these was potted; about half of the top growth was removed.

It was completely covered with polythene plastic and kept in a cold frame all winter, but as I expected it did not survive. Perhaps the reason for failure in this case was that the branches chosen for the layering were too large, or the layer was not started early enough.

Sometime in June a "tongue" is cut in the Rhododendron shoot to be layered and is dusted with Merck No. 3 Hormodin root-inducing powder. Under the tongue a little moist Sphagnum Moss is stuffed.

The whole is swaddled with a fist-size ball of moss.

It is then wrapped with sheet plastic, being careful to tie it in such a way that moisture cannot enter.

About October 1 the plastic is removed and if roots show good development, the moss is partly removed, with care given to avoid injury to the roots. The layer is cut off just below the root ball and the new plant is set in a cold frame to become established before winter sets in.

CHAPTER VII

Perennial vegetables

MOST vegetables are either annuals or biennials which are treated as annuals and raised from seed. The propagation of the most important perennial vegetables is described below.

Asparagus is started from seeds. They are planted in the spring in rows 18 inches apart, the seedlings thinned to 3 inches apart. The following spring they are set in their permanent position, and are spaced 18 inches apart in rows 4 feet apart. Wait two years before cutting.

Horse-radish is propagated by root cuttings 6 to 8 inches long—about ¼ inch in diameter. The side roots are taken off when the crop is dug in the fall and kept over winter, buried outdoors in soil. They are planted in the spring. In order to avoid planting them upside-down, the top of the cutting is cut off squarely and the lower end is trimmed to an angle of about 45°.

Rhubarb is propagated by division of rootstock in the fall or very early in the spring. See Peony, page 72, for techniques.

Sweet potatoes are propagated by means of rooted shoots which are called sets or slips. This is a root tuber from which shoots already are emerging.

Enough slips can be obtained for home use by starting them in a box similar to this one pictured—6 to 8 inches deep, 1 foot wide, and about 14 inches long, filled with moist peat moss and/or sand, or vermiculite.

After a few weeks' time there is a regular forest of shoots. The box containing these should be removed from the house and put in a cold frame or sheltered place for seven to ten days to harden off the shoots before planting them outdoors. When ready to plant in the outdoor garden, they are taken off by holding down the tuber with one hand and pulling off individual shoots with the other.

Do not, as a friend of mine did, pot up the slips before planting them. If you do, your crop probably will be like this instead of being similar to the one below.

Normal production of sweet potatoes. This is a small crop because it was grown so far north (in the mid-Hudson Valley), where the season was not long enough to produce a full crop.

White or "Irish" potatoes are propagated by underground stem tubers, either by cutting them into pieces, each one containing an eye, or, as is done in England, by planting the entire potato.

CHAPTER VIII

Graftage

THIS is the term used to describe the operation of placing or inserting a portion of one plant (bud or scion) upon another plant (the understock) so that they grow together. Budding usually is performed in the summer at a time when the understock is actively growing and the bark separates readily from the wood; grafting usually is done in winter, when the plants are dormant. There are many different reasons why graftage is practiced by horticulturists. Its chief use is in the propagation of plants that, because of their mixed ancestry, do not come true from seeds; plants that do not produce seed; or those that do not readily make roots from cuttings. Most of our fruit trees are in this group. Apples are budded or grafted on seedling Apple understocks, on young plants of special stocks propagated by layering, or on pieces or roots of older trees. Peaches are usually budded on seedlings of the "wild" Peach. Pears are budded or grafted on Pear seedlings or on Quince stocks obtained from cuttings or layers; and so on. The understock and scion must be related. For example, you cannot successfully graft an Apple on an Oak. See the list in the Appendix, page 234.

Graftage may be employed when a plant does not make satisfactory growth on its own roots, which explains why many nurserymen prefer to propagate by budding or grafting certain varieties of Roses and Azalea. It is a common practice among nurserymen to bud or graft named Lilacs on plants or cuttings of Privet. This practice has been condemned by some who claim that it renders the Lilacs subject to a disease known as "graft blight." It does, however, result in a salable plant in a shorter time, and, if grafted so that ultimately the Lilac may form its own root system, it is difficult to see any objection to the practice. In any case, it is preferable to working named Lilacs on seedling Lilacs, which are likely to sucker badly and choke out the scion, and because they are so much alike, it is practically impossible to distinguish the understock from the scion.

Graftage is used sometimes to adapt plants to soil conditions. For example: Plums, which thrive best in heavy clay soil, may be budded on Peach to enable them to grow in sandy soil. It is also used to help trees to withstand a severe climate, as when Apples are grafted on a rootstock of known hardiness.

The important thing to remember in graftage is that the cambium layer of the understock and that of the scion must be in contact. The cambium layer is a cylinder of actively growing cells between the wood and the bark. When the diameter of the understock is larger than that of the scion, or vice versa, it is necessary to put the scion toward one side to ensure that the contact is properly made. See the illustration on page 211.

Budding

If you have a pet Apple tree you wish to propagate—maybe it is one the name of which has been lost, or one like this one, which is dying, it is possible to give it a new lease of life by budding it on a suitable understock. This can be a seedling Apple tree you may be able to find somewhere on your grounds, or you can dig up a root of pencil thickness from an apple on which you can use a whip graft.

Here is a bud stick (right); on the left it is prepared for use by removing the leaves except for ½ inch of the leafstalk left on to serve as a handle.

The bud which is to form your future tree is being cut from the bud stick.

The lower leaves of a seedling understock are removed.

"T" or "shield" budding is the method commonly used. The first step is to make the transverse cut of the "T." The knife must be razor sharp, preferably with a rounded point (see drawing page 202). The cut should be made through the bark but not extending into the wood. A vertical cut is started about 1½ inches below the horizontal cut, as the latter is reached the blade is flicked, left and right, to raise flaps of bark at each corner of the cut.

A bud is slipped into the "T."

The bud inserted and tied in place with a rubber band. The advantage of using rubber as a tie is that it "gives" so that there is less danger of strangling the bud owing to increasing thickness of the understock.

Budding knives.

The following spring the bud has started to grow and the understock is cut off just above it.

Seven years later the bud has grown into a tree of flowering size. The only pruning this tree has experienced was done by rabbits the first year and deer the second and third years.

Hybrid Tea Roses usually are propagated by budding on seedlings or cuttings of a strong growing rose such as *Rosa multiflora* and the Ragged Robin. Seldom, however, does the amateur gardener have on hand understocks of this nature, but he may have a mature plant or two of *Rosa multiflora* which grew up from the understock (below-ground parts) of a grafted rose, or by chance may have a "living hedge" which will provide suitable material for budding in the cane. The climbing Rose, Dr. Huey, also has been used successfully and there may be others. Several buds can be inserted in one cane. These should be spaced far enough apart to permit the cane to be made into cuttings containing at least two or three nodes. The buds can be inserted any time when the bark of the understock lifts (separates) readily. This period usually occurs during July and August or during early spring. See the illustrations on pages 200–203 for details of budding.

The bud is tied in place with soft raffia, rubber "budding strips," or, as was done in this case, with a narrow strip of plastic film.

After a week or two the cuttings can be made. In order to prevent the development of suckers it is desirable to cut out the growth bud of that part of the understock which will be below ground.

Make the basal cut just below a joint.

The cuttings are inserted in a standard cutting mixture and kept in a closed and shaded cold frame or under constant mist.

A few weeks later roots have started to grow on the understock.

The inserted bud has started to grow.

The following spring the budded portion is blossoming. The understock is cut off quite close to the budded portion. This plant is one which was left untransplanted in the cutting frame. Ideally it should have been transplanted in the early spring. Notice the size and quality of the root system. Although it was not planted in the rose bed until June, late planting did not seem to harm it greatly.

One way of propagating Lilac is by budding it on cuttings of Privet during July and August. Preferably the cuttings should be of pencil thickness.

Grafting

There are many kinds of grafts, including whip, splice, saddle, wedge, side, and veneer. Of these the most important are the whip graft, sometimes called the "tongue" graft, and the side graft, or a modification of this called veneer graft. Then there is the cleft graft, which is used to make over fruit trees, an operation that is known as top-working.

Whip-grafting is commonly practiced in propagation of Cherry (both ornamental and fruit-bearing), Apple, Pear, etc.

The way to make a whip graft is as follows: the scion is cut to a length of 4 to 6 inches from a shoot which grew the preceding year.

With a sharp knife long sloping cuts are made on both scion and understock. This should be done with a single cut to insure a smooth surface.

Tongues are made in both by vertical cuts starting near the point of the diagonal cuts.

Stock and scion are then fitted together.

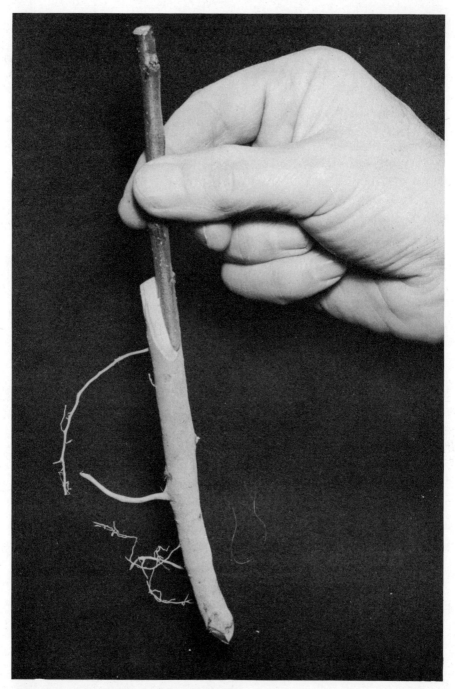

Here we see the tightly fitted joint with the cambium layers of scion and under-stock aligned at one side.

The finished graft tied together with thin cotton twine. Grafts of this kind are stored and treated the same as hardwood cuttings (see page 117).

This is a saddle graft of Lilac on Privet cutting. The base of the cutting and site of the graft have been dusted with a root-inducing powder. It was inserted in sand to the lowermost leaves and put under constant mist, but the union failed to take.

A saddle graft is made by cutting the understock to a long wedge shape; the scion is split and fitted over this wedge as shown at A. This kind of grafting is considered to be especially desirable in propagation of Lilac because the base of the scion is favorably situated to induce rooting. The Privet serves mainly as a nurse root as shown at B.

Probable causes of failure are: it was done at the wrong season (we know it can be done during winter on rooted cuttings of Privet), and/or the material from which the Privet cuttings were made was not fresh—it had been lying around for a week or more.

This is a side graft often used in propagation of Japanese Maples, also for evergreens—both broad and narrow-leaved kinds (conifers). A greenhouse is needed for good results, so, seeing that I've spoken of inexpensive equipment, inclusion here is largely academic.

The understock usually is a seedling of a related plant which has been potted during the preceding spring so that roots are thoroughly established when the time comes to graft on it during the winter. The understocks are stored in a cool greenhouse (40° to 45°) until three or four weeks before the actual grafting is to be done. They are then put in a temperature of 60 to 65 degrees to start root action. A slit is cut near the base of the understock; the scion is cut to a long wedge shape and is pushed down into the slit and tied in place. They are kept in a closed propagating case in the greenhouse until the grafts have taken. Then air is gradually admitted. The tops of the understocks are gradually cut back until they are entirely removed.

Grafting knives and chisels.

A cleft is made by means of a grafting chisel or a strong pruning knife. A club or wooden mallet is used to drive the chisel into the wood.

The cleft graft is used chiefly to change a fruit tree, such as Apple, to a better variety. Branches, preferably between 1 and 2 inches in diameter, are cut off squarely.

The scions are cut to a long wedge shape. The cleft is held open by the wedge of the chisel, the scions are inserted, the wedge is removed and the "spring" of the wood holds them in place.

All cut surfaces are covered with grafting wax.

This work is done in early spring when the buds of the under-stock are beginning to swell. It is desirable that the scions should be in a less advanced stage of growth than the understock. Therefore they are cut the preceding fall and are buried out of doors in a cold spot such as the north side of an unheated building.

The owner of this Apple tree (I think he said it was the variety "Delicious") wanted to change it to McIntosh, so it was cut back to three branches, in each of which scions were placed. The shoots originating on the trunk and branches below the grafts must be removed.

Grafting is frequently resorted to by cactus fanciers, either to display their pets more efficiently or because they do not thrive very well on their own roots.

A slit is made in the top of the understock of the Blue Candle Cactus (*Myrtillocactus geometrizans*) by means of a razor blade of the injector type.

The scion of Christmas Cactus (*Zygocactus truncatus*) is prepared for insertion by cutting a sliver from the base of the stem.

It is inserted in the slit previously made.

Then it is pinned in place with a cactus thorn. A rubber band is put around the understock to assist further in holding it.

Owing to exigencies of photography the graft did not take, so later the secondary shoot of the understock was grafted with a single joint of Christmas Cactus. This one was successful and within a few months had made the growth seen here. The very spiny little cactus on the left is an interloper. It is *Mamillaria elongata*. I had given the parent plant to a Mexican boy who expressed an interest in it, reserving for myself one shoot, which was "temporarily" placed in with the Myrtillocactus.

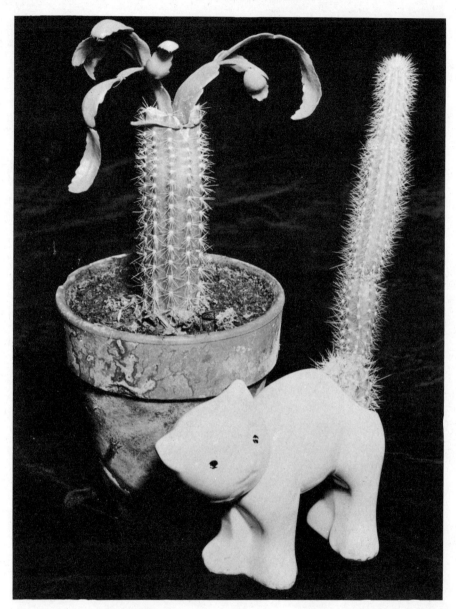

This ensemble resulted from a talk on "Fun with House Plants," which I gave at a garden-club meeting. The top of *Trichocereus Spachianus* was cut off and inserted in the rear end of the hollow, smug-looking cat, where it was intended to grow and form the animal's tail. Then the two scions of Zygocactus were wedge-grafted in the decapitated Trichocereus. The photograph was taken in 1949, about one year later. Since then the Trichocereus has provided several tails for similar cats—and even dogs!

Notocactus Haselbergi on Trichocereus.

Pilocereus "lanatus cristatus" grafted
on Cereus. In this type of graft
the top is sliced off the understock and the scion, similarly cut,
is put in place and held there by
cactus thorns and by tying.

Garden varieties of *Paeonia moutan* (Tree Peony), are notoriously difficult to propagate by means of cuttings. Because of this commercial Peony growers usually increase named varieties by means of grafting. The understock may be seedlings of *Paeonia moutan;* the wild form of Tree Peony; or pieces of roots of herbaceous Peony. The latter is preferred because it is easier to recognize the understock if it should happen to send up suckers. This shows scions of Tree Peony which have been grafted on pieces of root of herbaceous Peony.

When planting recently grafted Peonies such as these it is desirable to set them so that only the upper bud is above the ground.

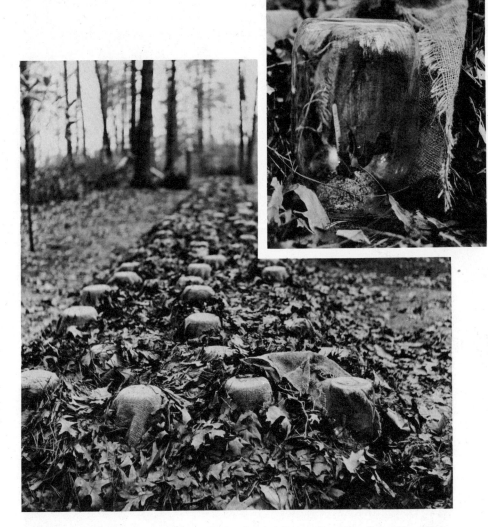

Propagating bed for Camellia varieties in public park at Norfolk, Va. Wide-mouth gallon jars are used by Mr. Fred Heutte the superintendent, to maintain a humid atmosphere around the grafts. The understocks are seedlings of Camellia which are cut back almost to the ground preparatory to grafting them in January in the vicinity of Mobile, Ala., and in February and March around Norfolk, Va. A wedge graft was used. As soon as the grafting is finished, the jars are put in place, covered with burlap, and the whole bed is mulched with a 6-inch layer of leaves. When there is evidence that the grafts have "taken," the burlap is removed and air is gradually admitted to the grafts by tilting the jars.

CHAPTER IX

Rooting mediums and equipment

ALMOST any moisture-holding substance can be used as a rooting medium for cuttings. Among those favored by experienced propagators are: sand, peat moss, Sphagnum moss, vermiculite, perlite, polystyrene, and mixtures of these in various proportions; then there is the 1-1-1 mixture of garden soil, sand, and peat moss or leaf mold, in favor forty or fifty years ago, which has the advantage of containing some plant nutrients and can be used for starting seeds as well as cuttings. Just plain sand works well with a large number of species, that is, if the right kind—coarse, sharp, and porous—is obtained and is watered frequently. The chief disadvantage of sand is its great weight if it is contained in flats which have to be moved occasionally. Sand and peat moss combined, equal parts of each by bulk, are good especially for those plants which require an acid soil. Vermiculite is a lightweight material which is valuable because the roots produced in it are, in the case of Taxus at least, much less brittle than those rooted in sand. Perlite and vermiculite, equal parts of each, have been used with success. Some plants root with greater ease with one or the other of these materials.

To begin with, I would suggest a mixture of sand and peat moss in proportion of about 75 per cent sand and 25 per cent peat moss, or just sand. For seeds (and some cuttings) it is better to use a mixture of equal parts sand, peat moss, and garden soil (the 1-1-1 mixture). This should be surfaced with a half inch of sand, some of which is pushed down with the dibber into the medium to provide a well-drained and aerated spot at the base of the cutting. If you have the time and are interested, you could amuse yourself by experimenting with other rooting mediums. When soil is contained in the rooting medium, it is desirable to "sterilize" it separately, either chemically or by heating it to about 180° Fahrenheit for half an hour or so.

One of the best all-around mediums is a mixture of sand and peat moss. In the picture peat moss contained in the pail is being moistened preparatory to mixing it with the sand.

Proportions of sand and peat moss vary. Here we have a ratio of about ten parts sand to one part peat moss.

The peat moss and sand must be thoroughly mixed. A good place to do this is in a steel-tray wheelbarrow.

The 1-1-1 mixture of equal parts garden soil, sand, and peat moss is put through a ¼-inch-mesh sieve. The coarse material, which does not pass through the sieve, is known as "rough stuff." It can be used in the bottom of flats or pots to help drainage when rooted cuttings are being "flatted" or potted.

Here is vermiculite being filled into a box which has a 2-inch layer of coarse sand in the bottom to help drainage. One advantage of vermiculite is its light weight.

If you are interested in raising a small number of cuttings of different kinds of plants, flowerpots are preferred to a bed in a cold frame or on a greenhouse bench. You see, some kinds root more quickly than others and should be hardened off as soon as they have rooted, which can be done without disturbing the remainder when they are in individual pots. The next best thing is to use metal, plastic, or wooden flats about 10 by 14 by 4 inches. The last-named should be treated with copper naphthenate (Cuprinol), which helps to prevent decay of the wood.

The use of Sphagnum moss for seed germination and for rooting cuttings is a comparatively recent development. It is claimed that its use practically eliminates danger of seedlings being attacked by damping-off fungi. Sphagnum is a moss which is commonly found growing in bogs. Probably you can buy a quantity sufficient for your needs from your florist. It is often used by florists to provide a base for funeral wreaths, and if you are unable to purchase it locally, you can probably get a quantity by raiding a cemetery dump.

It is prepared for seed sowing by drying it and then rubbing it through a sieve, which can be made by tacking to a frame a piece of hardware cloth with three meshes to the inch. It is then moistened and packed evenly in a small flat, watered thoroughly, and an additional thin layer of Sphagnum is put on the surface. The seeds are sown on the surface and sprinkled lightly with water applied as a fine spray. The flat is then covered with glass or a piece of polythene film on a wooden frame that is fitted exactly on the rim of the flat. Usually no watering is required for two or three weeks, by which time most of the seeds will have germinated. As soon as this occurs, the covering should be removed and the seedlings gradually inured to ample light. The method is fully described in *Farmers Bulletin,* No. 2085, U. S. Department of Agriculture, which can be obtained for ten cents from the Superintendent of Documents, Washington 25, D.C.

Shredded moist Sphagnum is rounded above the rim of a galvanized asphalt-painted metal flat. (A plastic or wooden flat can be used if more convenient.) A float is used to press it down evenly to ½ inch below the rim.

The flat has been prepared for sowing seeds, the moss has been saturated with water, seeds have been sown on the surface of Sphagnum and covered with a pane of glass laid on a spacer frame. Instead of the glass a sheet of plastic film could be tacked to the frame.

Seedlings can be kept in a state of suspended animation for a long period. Here are two flats of Cinchona seedlings, about twelve months old. Those on the right were taken from the flat on the left two months previously. Sphagnum can also be used for propagating plants vegetatively by stem, root, and leaf cuttings.

Begonia leaf cutting showing new plantlets.

Leaf-bud cutting of Camellia.

A sharp knife is necessary for making cuttings and in budding or grafting. A kitchen paring knife, if properly honed, will serve in a pinch. If you are planning to top-work fruit trees, you will need either a grafting chisel or a knife with a heavy blade which won't break when it is hammered into the understock. Special budding and grafting knives are, of course, preferred (see page 210). You will need tying materials when budding and grafting is practiced. For budding you can use raffia if it is moistened to make it pliable; or rubber budding strips, which can be made quite easily from rubber bands; or plastic film cut into strips about ¼ inch wide. If raffia is used, it is necessary to cut through it on the side opposite the bud after two or three weeks. This is to prevent strangulation of the bud by the increase in girth of the understock. For grafting, thin, soft twine which disintegrates in contact with moisture is desirable for tying side and whip grafts in place.

A small cold frame also is desirable. This can be purchased ready-made, or one can easily be made by using scrap lumber like the one pictured on page 101, which was made to fit a discarded window sash. The back should be about 18 inches high and the front 12 inches. The two ends are made by cutting a 6-inch-wide piece of lumber diagonally to give the desired slope. If you don't want to go to the trouble or expense of making a cold frame of this size, you can get by with an old Apple box or something similar with the top and bottom knocked out. This should be placed on the ground so that there is a slight slope from back to front, with a cover of glass or of translucent plastic film tacked onto the wood frame of lumber 1 by 1 inch cut to fit.

A standard cold frame 3 by 6 feet can be made into a hotbed by installing an electric heating cable. This with a thermostat will cost about $7.00. The bottom heat it provides is desirable, but you can get along without it.

You will need two sieves, one with ¼- or ⅜-inch mesh, the other with a mesh of ⅛ inch. The first can easily be obtained by buying a small portion of hardware cloth from your dealer. He will, I am sure, cut it to the exact size you want it so that it can be tacked or stapled to a frame made of lumber 1 by 4 inches.

This is Ralph Bailey's 4-foot-wide propagating frame with the sash removed. On the left are *Campanula medium* (Canterbury Bells) and *Digitalis purpurea* (Foxglove), which were sown at the end of June and transplanted to the cold frame in July. They were photographed late in September. These can be planted in their flowering positions in the fall or left as they are until spring, depending on the severity of the climate. At the right there are various late-sown, recently transplanted perennials which are not big enough to be put in their permanent locations.

The over-all dimensions should be about 12 by 15 by 4 inches. The small-mesh sieve can be made from wire fly screening. The frame for this can be smaller than the preceding one, say about 6 by 9 by 3 inches.

A float is needed to compress soil or Sphagnum in the flats. This can be about 6 by 4 by 1 inches made with a handle. You will notice on page 139 that I have used a section of flooring with two screw hooks put in to serve as a handle. For tamping soil in pots a smooth-bottomed glass tumbler or a section of a tree branch about 2 inches in diameter can be used.

Fluorescent lighting

So far the equipment costs have been practically nothing. But if you want some of the refinements, such as fluorescent lighting, you will not have to dig too deeply in your pocketbook. The setup I put in my cellar cost about $28 for two 40-watt lights and a timer which turns the lights on about 8 A.M. and shuts them off at 9 P.M. This just about took care of the expense. In this particular case appearance did not matter. All that was required was that it should be functional. An old kitchen table was set up on a low platform made with boards and sawhorses. Two pieces of lumber 2 by 4 by 48 inches were laid on the table to support four aluminum trays, each 17½ by 11½ by 1 inches, in which the pots, etc., were placed. A roll of aluminum foil provided an effective reflector. This was supported on a piece of lumber 48 by 1 by 1 inches, which was held 8 inches from the wall by two brackets. Aluminum foil 17 inches wide was cut into three lengths extending from below the trays over the bar and then over the fixture itself, thus enclosing the whole setup except for the ends, which were left open. When it is necessary to care for the plants, the foil is just thrown up over the top, and then, when the job is finished, the flaps are brought down again to the original position.

Another advantage of the reflector is that it helps to maintain the temperature three or four degrees higher than outside. Also the humidity is increased from 10 to 20 per cent because the evaporation of moisture is confined to some extent. This was set up in our cellar, where the temperature in winter hovers around 60°. If yours happens to run cooler than this during the winter months, it would be desirable to install, in addition to the fluorescent lights, one or two tungsten lamps, which probably would be enough to raise the temperature 10° or 15°.

This really worked out very successfully, especially with leaf cuttings of Saintpaulia, which reached flowering size weeks ahead of those which were kept in my study, where the lighting is natural. There was one plant, a Poinsettia, which definitely resented being in this enclosure. It was a healthy plant when it was brought in. Its flower buds were already visible, but after about three weeks it showed signs of deterioration and by Christmas was a wreck.

Fluorescent lighting in author's cellar.

If you want something a little more fancy than the preceding, here is an arrangement from the U. S. Department of Agriculture. It is equipped with a heating unit to provide bottom heat. It is desirable, although not absolutely necessary, to maintain a temperature of the rooting medium 5° to 10° higher than that of the air. The front of the case is hinged so that it can be swung back. Camellia cuttings are in the center flat.

Working plan showing the false bottom to accommodate the heating unit.

Appendix

PROPAGATION NOTEBOOK

Inserted May 17

KIND	ROOTED	REMARKS
		(Note: s. stands for sand; p.m. and s. stands for peat moss and sand)
Neillia sinensis	June 10	Remarkably quick rooting.

Inserted June 8

KIND	ROOTED	REMARKS
Corylopsis pauciflora	Sept. 1	No difference caused by position of cuts.
Corylopsis spicata	Sept. 1	Better in p.m. and s. with cut made between nodes.
Cytisus praecox	July 21	Current-season shoots only rooted. No difference, s. and p.m. and s.
Daphne genkwa	Aug. 10	Best in sand. Root cuttings preferred.
Fothergilla major	July 22	Better in p.m. and s. with cut made between nodes.
Syringa vulgaris	Aug. 3	In s. only. No roots in p.m. and s.
Parrotia persica	Aug. 17	No difference in s. and p.m. and s. No difference in position of cut.
Polygala Dalmaisiana	July 27	Best in p.m. and. s.
Stachyurus chinensis	Sept. 11 (30%)	Better in s.
Poncirus trifoliatus	Aug. 3	Better in p.m. and s.

Inserted June 15

KIND	ROOTED	REMARKS
Azalea species	Aug. 3	Better roots in p.m. and s.
Azalea daviesi	Aug. 17 (100%)	P.m. and s. best.
Azalea hinodegiri	Aug. 17 (100%)	In s. and p.m. and s., but better roots in latter.
Berberis verruculosa	July 24 (1 of 6)	In s. All dead in p.m. and s.
Crape-myrtle	July 21 (100%)	Better roots in p.m. and s.
Jasminum nudiflorum	July 21	Best in p.m. and s.
Osmanthus aquifolium	Aug. 3 (100%)	Best in s. No difference in position of cut.

KIND	ROOTED	REMARKS
Pieris japonica	Aug. 10	Heel cuttings; p.m. and s. best.
Salix babylonica annularis	Aug. 10 (75%)	Too soft.
Tamarix odessana	————	Did not root. Too early.
Tamarix pentandra	————	(See Inserted July 7)
Taxus brevifolia	Sept. 26 (100%)	Rooted more quickly in s. Best results in p.m. and s.
Viburnum Carlesi	Aug. 3	P.m. and s. best. Those in s. alive but unrooted Sept. 12.

Inserted June 19

Buxus sempervirens	Sept. 26 (100%)	Both old and young wood. Best in s.
Cotoneaster horizontalis	Aug. 3 (100%)	Best in p.m. and s.
Thuja occidentalis	Sept. 26 (50%)	Best in p.m. and s.
Thuja orientalis	Sept. 26 (100%)	Best in p.m. and s.

Inserted June 28

Viburnum tomentosum	Aug. 10	Did better than June 15 insertions. 100% rooted in s. Heel cuttings; or cut through "rings" on stem better than below nodes.

Inserted July 7

Corylopsis Willmottiae	Sept. 11 (50%)	Best in p.m. and s.
Magnolia stellata	Sept. 26 (20%)	P.m. and s. and cut between nodes.
Tamarix odessana	July 27	P.m. and s. Earlier insertions did
Tamarix parviflora	July 27	not root.
Viburnum utile	Aug. 17 (100%)	In s.

Inserted July 17

Daphne cneorum	Sept. 1 (100%)	In s.

Inserted July 25

Azalea hinodegiri	Sept. 6 (100%)	Two-year wood rooted as easily as that of current season.
Berberis Julianae	Sept. 5 (100%)	No difference s. and p.m. and s. Cut between nodes better.
Berberis Neuberti	Sept. 5 (100%)	P.m. and s. best—slower in s. Cut between nodes best.

KIND	ROOTED	REMARKS
Berberis verruculosa	Sept. 5	Same result as June 15.
Mahonia aquifolium	Sept. 5 (100%)	Cut between nodes. P.m. and s. gave rooting twenty days earlier.
Viburnum tomentosum	Sept. 1 (100%)	P.m. and s. Better than earlier insertions.

Inserted July 28

Chamaecyparis plumosa	Sept. 26 (50%)	Roots in p.m. and s. two weeks earlier than in s.

Inserted August 4

Rosa Rouletti	Sept. 1 (100%)	No difference s. and p.m. and s. or position of cuts.
Rosa chinensis viridiflora	Sept. 6 (100%)	P.m. and s. best.

Inserted August 10

Berberis verruculosa	Oct. 3	100% rooted in p.m. and s. Those in s. alive but not rooted.
Hydrangea Pee Gee	Aug. 31	Well rooted in p.m. and s. Those in s. barely started.
Pieris japonica	Sept. 26	100% p.m. and s.

A study of the preceding table will show that there are queer variations in the behavior of cuttings (notice especially *Berberis verruculosa*), caused by time of insertion, position of cuts, and kind of rooting medium, all of which tend to make the whole process of absorbing interest.

UNDERSTOCKS AND SCIONS

It is necessary for success in grafting that the understock and the scion be compatible, which means that they must be related botanically. Following is a list of plants and the understocks on which they may be grafted. The understocks usually are raised from seeds, occasionally from cuttings and layers.

Apple (dwarf)	Malling IX
Azalea	*A. ponticum*
Camellia	*C. japonica*
Catalpa	*C. speciosa*
Citrus (Orange, Grapefruit, Tangerine)	Sour Orange and Pomelo
Cornus (Flowering Dogwood)	*C. florida*

Cydonia (Flowering Quince)	C. japonica
Cydonia (Quince)	Common Quince
Malus (Apple)	Common Varieties
	French Crab Apple
Malus (Flowering Crab Apple)	Common Apple
Pear (dwarf)	Quince
Picea (Spruce)	Norway Spruce
Pinus (Pine)	
2-needle	P. sylvestris
5-needle	P. strobus
Prunus (Apricot)	Common Apricot
Prunus (Cherry-sour)	Mahaleb
Prunus (Cherry-sweet)	Black Mazzard
Prunus (Peach)	Wild from Kentucky and Tennessee
Prunus (Plum)	Myrobalan Plum
Pyracantha (Firethorn)	Crataegus
Pyrus (Pear)	Chinese or Japanese sand pear
Rosa	R. multiflora and others
Syringa—Lilac	Privet, Lilac
Taxus—Yew	T. cuspidata

PLANTS WHICH ROOTED BY AIR-LAYERING[1]

	NUMBER TRIED	NUMBER ROOTED		NUMBER TRIED	NUMBER ROOTED
*Abeliophyllum distichum	1	1	Acer platanoides var.	4	4
Abeliophyllum distichum	4	2	Acer saccharum monumentale	8	1
Acer barbinerve	6	4	Aesculus carnea	4	2
Acer capillipes	3	2	Aesculus hippocastanum	6	2
Acer circinatum	5	3	Aesculus hippocastanum		
Acer cissifolium	1	1	umbraculifera	4	1
Acer duretti	3	1	*Albizzia julibrissin rosea	10	5
Acer ginnala	2	1	Betula aurata	3	1
*Acer griseum	3	1	Betula fontinalis	4	2
Acer griseum	3	1	Carya tomentosa	6	1
Acer grosseri hessi	4	3	Castanea mollissima	10	1
Acer palmatum dissectum	4	1	Catalpa bignonioides	4	4
Acer pensylvanicum	6	6	Catalpa bungei	4	1
*Acer platanoides	6	4	Catalpa speciosa	4	2
Acer platanoides	4	1	Cercis chinensis	4	2
Acer platanoides globosum	4	3	Cladrastis platycarpa	3	2
Acer platanoides nanum	2	2	Clethra barbinervis	3	2

*Layers made in 1950, all others in 1951.

[1]Reprinted from THE ARNOLD ARBORETUM GARDEN BOOK, with permission of Arnold Arboretum, Boston, Mass.

	NUMBER TRIED	NUMBER ROOTED		NUMBER TRIED	NUMBER ROOTED
*Cornus alba sibirica	3	3	Malus prunifolia rinki	6	3
Cornus florida rubra	9	8	Malus purpurea	4	3
Corylopsis glabrescens	4	3	Malus sargenti rosea	6	3
Corylopsis spicata	4	3	Malus spectabilis	6	5
Corylus chinensis	4	1	Malus sublobata	6	6
*Cotinus coggygria purpureus	4	4	Malus "Wabiskaw"	4	2
Cotinus coggygria purpureus	11	3	Morus alba pendula	4	2
Cotoneaster foveolata	4	4	Orixa japonica	4	4
Cotoneaster horizontalis	4	4	Osmaronia cerasiformis	4	2
Crataegus monogyna stricta	6	1	*Populus alba nivea	2	2
Crataegus pinnatifida major	6	1	Prunus juddi	1	1
Cytisus praecox	4	1	Prunus maacki	2	2
Cytisus supinus	4	4	Prunus serrulata "Amanogawa"	4	3
Davidia involucrata vilmorini	15	5	Prunus serrulata "Gyoiko"	2	1
Diospyros lotus	4	2	Prunus serrulata Kwanzan	6	2
Enkianthus campanulatus	5	3	Prunus yedoensis "Taizanfukun"	4	4
*Forsythia "Arnold Dwarf"	3	3	Ptelea trifoliata aurea	6	2
Franklinia alatamaha	4	4	*Rhododendron "Dr. Charles		
Ginkgo biloba	1	1	Baumann"	7	5
Halesia carolina	6	6	*Rhododendron "Josephine Klinger"	9	8
Halesia monticola rosea	4	4	Salix caprea	7	7
Hedera helix baltica	4	4	Styrax japonica	7	2
*Hibiscus syriacus rosea	1	1	Symplocos paniculata	6	3
Hippophae rhamnoides	6	3	Syringa amurensis japonica	6	1
Ilex crenata convexa	4	4	Syringa prestoniae "Lucetta"	4	3
Ilex glabra	6	6	Syringa prestoniae "Paulina"	5	3
Ilex montana macropoda	1	1	Syringa villosa	5	3
Ilex verticillata	3	1	Syringa vulgaris vars.	35	9
Indigofera amblyantha	4	3	Tamarix pentandra	2	2
Koelreuteria paniculata	8	8	Taxus cuspidata nana	3	1
Laburnum anagyroides	4	3	Tilia cordata	5	3
Laburnum watereri	8	4	Tilia platyphyllos fastigiata	8	2
*Ligustrum ibota aureum	3	3	Tsuga canadensis	3	3
*Ligustrum ovalifolium	4	4	Ulmus carpinifolia koopmanni	6	1
Ligustrum vulgare buxifolium	4	4	Ulmus carpinifolia sarniensis	4	1
Lonicera maacki	4	2	Ulmus glabra	4	1
Maackia amurensis	4	4	Vaccinium corymbosum "Jersey"	3	2
Magnolia denudata	10	1	Virburnum carlesi	4	1
Magnolia soulangeana			*Viburnum dilatatum	4	1
"Alexandrina"	4	1	Viburnum juddi	4	1
Malus astracanica	4	1	*Viburnum opulus	2	2
Malus atrosanguinea	5	4	Viburnum rhytidophyllum	4	1
Malus "Dorothea"	5	5	Viburnum rufidulum	6	1
Malus floribunda	6	1	*Viburnum sargenti	6	5
Malus halliana spontanea	5	1	Viburnum sargenti	3	3
Malus "McIntosh"	3	2	Viburnum sargenti flavum	4	4
Malus micromalus	7	2	Viburnum setigerum aurantiacum	8	3

	NUMBER TRIED	NUMBER ROOTED		NUMBER TRIED	NUMBER ROOTED
Viburnum sieboldi	4	1	Wisteria macrostachya	4	4
Wisteria floribunda violacea-plena	4	2	Wisteria sinensis	15	1
Wisteria floribunda longissima			Wisteria sinensis hybrid	2	2
alba	4	2	Wisteria venusta	3	1
Wisteria floribunda "Naga Noda"	4	4	Zelkova serrata	6	6
Wisteria formosa	4	2	Zelkova sinica	6	3

PLANTS WHICH FAILED TO ROOT BY AIR-LAYERING

	NUMBER OF LAYERS TRIED		NUMBER OF LAYERS TRIED
Abies homolepis umbellata	6	Crataegus coccinioides	6
Acer campstre	6	Crataegus lavallei	4
Acer palmatum atropurpureum	1	Crataegus monogyna inermis	2
Acer palmatum lutescens	2	Crataegus monogyna versicolor	3
Acer platanoides	6	Crataegus nitida	5
Acer shirasawanum	3	Crataegus pruinosa	6
Acer tataricum	6	Crataegus punctata	6
Aesculus carnea plantierensis	5	Crataegus succulenta	3
Aesculus discolor mollis	4	Diospyros virginiana	4
Aesculus glabra leucodermis	4	Eucommia ulmoides	4
Albizzia julibrissin rosea	16	Evodia danielli	4
Amelanchier canadensis	2	Fagus grandifolia	2
Amelasorbus jacki	4	Fagus sylvatica atropunicea	3
Betula jacquemontiana	3	Fagus sylvatica pendula	4
Carpinus cordata	4	Fothergilla monticola	2
Carpinus orientalis	4	Fraxinus chinensis	6
Carya glabra	6	Fraxinus pennsylvanicum	4
Carya laneyi	2	Gleditsia triacanthos	6
Carya ovata	4	Gleditsia triacanthos inermis	4
Carya schnecki	4	Hamamelis mollis	8
Castanea dentata	4	*Hamamelis mollis	3
Catalpa fargesi	6	Juglans cinerea	6
Cercis canadensis alba	8	Juglans nigra	9
Chaenomeles sinensis	4	*Juglans nigra laciniata	4
Chionanthus retusa	4	Juglans nigra laciniata	5
Chionanthus virginicus	2	Kalmia latifolia	5
Cladrastic lutea	4	Kalmia latifolia polypetala	7
Cornus florida	4	Kalopanax pictus	4
Cornus mas elegantissima	8	Linderabenzoin	3
Cornus officinalis	4	Magnolia fraseri	6
Corylus avellana fusco-rubra	4	Magnolia loebneri	6
Corylus avellana contorta	3	*Magnolia stellata rosea	4
Corylus colurna	5	Magnolia stellata rosea	6
Cotinus americanus	5	Magnolia virginiana	4
Crataegus arnoldiana	4	Malus "Arrow"	3

	NUMBER OF LAYERS TRIED		NUMBER OF LAYERS TRIED
Malus baccata	5	Quercus runcinata	6
Malus "Bob White"	4	Quercus stellata	5
Malus brevipes	1	Quercus variabilis	4
Malus coronaria charlottae	3	Rhododendron "Mrs. C. S. Sargent"	4
Malus florentina	5	Rhododendron "Purpureum	
Malus glabrata	4	grandiflorum"	2
Malus hupehensis	5	Rhododendron "Watereri"	3
Malus ioensis plena	1	Robinia longiloba	3
Malus robusta	4	Sophora japonica	4
Malus sargenti	6	Sorbus alnifolia	4
Parrotia persica	4	Sorbus aria	4
Phellodendron amurense	9	Sorbus aucuparia	8
Phellodendron chinensis	4	Sorbus latifolia	6
Phellodendron sachalinensis	6	Sorbus matsumarana	4
Photinia villosa	4	Sorbus pratti	3
Pinus bungeana	5	Sorbus thuringiaca	4
Prunus maritima "Eastham"	4	Syringa pubescens	4
Prunus maritima "Raribank"	4	Taxus cuspidata expansa	4
Prunus serrulata	5	Thuja standishi	5
Pseudolarix amabilis	4	Tilia americana fastigiata	4
Quercus bebbiana	4	Tilia platyphyllos	6
Quercus bicolor	6	Tsuga caroliniana	4
Quercus dentata	4	Ulmus carpinifolia dampieri	4
Quercus falcata	3	Ulmus carpinifolia umbraculifera	6
Quercus marilandica	5	Ulmus carpinifolia wredi	4
Quercus mongolica	5	Ulmus plotti	4
Quercus robur	6	Vaccinium corymbosum "Harding"	2
Quercus robur argenteo marginata	4	Wisteria "Jako"	2

Index

Abrasives (in rooting cuttings), 138
Abscission layer
  defined, 13
  of Willow, 13
Abutilon
  cutting of, 83
Acanthus, 133
Aesculus parviflora (Bottlebrush Buck-
  eye), 133
African-violet. *See* Saintpaulia
Air-borne seeds. *See* Seeds, distribu-
  tion of
Air-layering. *See* Layering
Airplane-plant (*Chlorophytum elatum*),
  177, 179
Air-plant, 121
Air-wrap (root-inducing hormone),
  190
Ajuga reptans (Creeping Bugle),
  178
Albizzia Julibrissin ("Mimosa"), 133
Alkanet (Anchusa), 133
Alternanthera, 94
Althaea rosea (Hollyhock), 19
Alyssum saxatile, 136
American Iris Society Bulletin, 47
Anchusa (Alkanet), 133
Anemone
  Japanese, 132, 134
Anemone hupehensis, 133
  japonica, 133, 134
Animals
  and distribution of seeds, 18, 22
Annuals (hardy)
  planting of, 19
  seeds of, 19

Antheridia, 48
Apostle-plant (*Neomarica Northiana*),
  177
Apple
  budding of, 198, 199ff.
  "Delicious," 213
  dwarfing understock for, 53
  grafting of, 198, 199, 207, 212
  McIntosh, 213
Aquilegia caerulea, 19
 chrysantha, 19
Arabis, 136
Arbor-vitae (*Thuja*), 17
  cuttings of, 111
Arbutus
  Trailing (*Epigaea repens*), 107
Archegonia, 48
Arnold Arboretum, 184
Arnold Arboretum Garden Book, 139
Artichoke
  Jerusalem, 156
Asexual (vegetative) propagation,
  11–12, 53–77
Ash (tree)
  seeds of, 40
Asparagus, 195
Aspidistra, 60
Asplenium ebenoides (Scott's Spleen-
  wort), 48, 50, 51
 platyneuron (Ebony Spleenwort),
  48, 50
Aster
  Hardy (*Aster novi-belgi*), 54, 120,
  136–37
Avocado
  seed of, 25

Azalea (Rhododendron)
cuttings of, 96
grafting of, 198
seed of, 40

Babys-breath (Gypsophila), 133
Bailey, Ralph, 228
Balloon-flower (Platycodon), 19
Barberry
cuttings of, 96, 97
seed of, 40
Beauty-bush (*Kolkwitzia amabilis*)
cuttings of, 106
Bedding plants, 94
Beggars Tick
seed of, 17
Begonia, 26, 28, 31, 78, 156
seed of, 17, 49, 170
Tuberous, 167–70
Begonia Rex
leaf cutting of, 128
Bellis perennis (English Daisy), 19
Bernard, Noel, 36
Berry
Turquoise, 18
Bete fog nozzle, 146
Biennials
planting of, 19
Birds
and distribution of seeds, 18, 19, 22
Bittersweet (Celastrus), 133
Bleeding-heart, 19
Bloodleaf (Iresine), 78
Bocconia cordata (Plume-poppy),19,133
Botrytis disease, 73
Bottlebrush Buckeye (*Aesculus parvi-flora*), 133
Bouvardia
"Bridesmaid," 53, 134
Boxwood (*Buxus sempervirens rotundi-folia*)
cuttings of, 96, 118
Brazil Nut
seed of, 17

Bromelia lasiantha, 178
Bromeliad
seed of, 17
runners of, 178
Broom
Early (*Cytisus praecox*), 141–43, 152, 153, 154
Budding, 12, 198, 199–200
equipment for, 227
Buddleia
cuttings of, 104
Buddleia alternifolia (Garland Butter-fly-bush), 98, 106
Bugle
Creeping (*Ajuga reptans*), 178
Bulbils, 12
described, 156
propagation by, 12
stem, 161
Bulblets, 12, 157, 163
described, 156
propagation by, 12
Bulbs, 155, 156–63
Burdock
seed of, 17
Buxus sempervirens rotundifolia (Box-wood)
cuttings of, 96, 118

Cactus
Blue Candle (*Myrtillocactus geo-metrizans*), 214, 215
Christmas (*Zygocactus truncatus*), 214, 215, 216
grafting of, 214–17
Callus, 151
Calycanthus (Sweet-shrub), 133
Cambium layer
in graftage, 199
Camellia, 148, 230
leaf-bud cutting of, 226
varieties, 219
Campanula isophylla (Ligurian Hare-bell), 79
medium (Canterbury Bells), 19, 228

Campanula isophylla (cont.)
  medium calycanthema (Cup-and-saucer Bells), 19
Campsis (Trumpet-creeper), 133
Camptosorus rhizophyllus (Walking Fern), 48, 49
Canna, 156
  seed of, 17
Canterbury Bells (*Campanula medium*), 19, 228
Cast-iron-plant. *See* Aspidistra
Catalpa (Indian-bean), 133
  seed of, 17
Cattleya Trianaei, 20
Celastrus (Bittersweet), 133
Cereus, 217
Cereus Spachianus, 35
Chamaecyparis (False Cypress), 17
  cuttings of, 96
Cheiranthus Cheiri (Wallflower), 19
Cherry
  whip-grafting of, 207
Chestnut
  seed of, 40
Chlorophytum elatum (Spider-plant, Airplane-plant), 177, 179
Christmas-rose (Helleborus), 19
Chrysanthemum
  cuttings of, 136–37
  division of, 54
  varieties of, 19
Cinchona, 225
Cladrastis (Yellow-wood), 133
Clerodendron (Glory Bower), 133
Cold frame
  construction of, 227
  and layering, 184, 194
  and root cuttings, 132
  and tree, shrub cuttings, 96ff.
Coleus
  cuttings of, 83, 88
Columbine (Aquilegia)
  species of, 19
Conifers
  seeds of, 40

Constant mist, 53
  and leaf-bud cuttings, 131
  and rooting cuttings, 144–54
Coreopsis, 19
Coreopsis tinctoria (Golden Shower), 67–68, 71
Cormels, 12, 164
Corms, 12, 155–56, 164
  described, 155
Cornell University, 36
Cornus stolonifera (Red-osier Dogwood), 177
Cosper, L. C., 36
Cotoneaster
  seed of, 40, 41
Crab Apple
  seed of, 45–46
Crinum
  seed of, 17
Crocus, 155
Cryptomeria
  cuttings of, 97
Cup-and-saucer Bells (*Campanula medium calycanthema*), 19
Cuprinol (copper naphthenate), 44, 223
Cuttings (propagation by)
  and air, 89
  and constant mist, 53, 131, 144–54
  of deciduous shrubs, 116–17
  of hardy shrubs and trees, 96–115
  of house plants, 78–95
  leaf, 121–29
  leaf-bud, 128–31, 226, 229–30
  rooting mediums and equipment for, 220–31
  softwood, of shrubs and trees, 97–110
  stem (Begonia), 167–69
  techniques for rooting, 53, 116, 138–43, 220–31
  water-rooted, 93
  see also: Graftage; Moisture; Soil; Temperature
Cyclamen, 156

Cytisus praecox (Early Broom), 141–43, 152, 153, 154

Daffodil, 157
Dahlia, 156
Daisy
    English (*Bellis perennis*), 19
    Michaelmas, 120
Dandelion
    seed of, 17
Daphne
    cuttings of, 96, 153
    Rose (*Daphne Cneorum*), 149
Day-lily, 69
Delphinium, 136
Dianthus, 136
Dianthus barbatus (Sweet William), 19
Dictamnus (Gas-plant), 19
Diervilla
    cuttings of, 96
Digitalis purpurea (Foxglove), 19, 228
Distribution of seeds
    by animals, 18
    by birds, 18, 19, 22
    by insects, 19
    means of, 17–18
Division of plants, 12, 53, 54–77; *see also* Chapters IV and V
Dr. Huey (Climbing Rose), 204
Dogwood (Cornus)
    air-layering of, 191
    Kousa, 42–43
    pink-flowering, 154
    Red-osier (*Cornus stolonifera*), 177
    seed of, 40
Donkey's Tail (*Sedum Morganianum*), 123

Echeveria, 94, 125
Echeveria microcalyx, 85
    Weinbergi, 125
Echinops (Globe-thistle), 133
Embryo, 48
    excision of, 12, 45–47
Empress Tree (Paulownia), 133
    seed of, 17

Enkianthus
    layering of, 188
    seed of, 40
Epigaea repens (Trailing Arbutus), 107
Equipment, tools, 220–31
Euonymus
    seed of, 40
Euonymus Fortunei
    cuttings of, 103
    vegetus, 104
    Kiautschovica
        cuttings of, 104
        (*patens*), 106
Evening-primrose (Oenothera), 134
Explosive fruits, 18

False Cypress (*Chamaecyparis*), 17
Farmers Bulletin (U. S. Department of Agriculture), 224
Fern, 48–51
    hybrid, 48–50
    Walking (*Camptosorus rhizophyllus*), 48, 49, 50
Fir
    seed of, 40
Flax
    Perennial, 19
Floaters (seeds)
    aerial, 17
    in water, 17
Floppers, 121
Fluorescent lighting, 229–30
Fog box. *See* Constant mist
Forget-me-not (Myosotis), 19
"Forsyth" cutting pot, 89
Forsythia
    cuttings of, 96
Foxglove (*Digitalis purpurea*), 19, 228
Fruit trees. *See under* Trees
Fuchsia
    cuttings of, 83

Galium
    seed of, 18

Garland Butterfly-bush (*Buddleia alternifolia*)
cuttings of, 98, 106
Gas-plant (Dictamnus), 19
Gay Feather (Liatris), 19
Geranium
House (Pelargonium), 53, 81–82, 134
Germination
and excision of the embryo, 45
and handling of seeds, 12
and moisture, 17, 18, 26, 30, 32, 224
and temperature, 18–19, 40
Gladiolus, 155, 164
Gliders (seeds), 17
Globe-flower (Trollius), 134
Globe-thistle (Echinops), 133
Gloriosa Rothschildiana, 165
Glory Bower (Clerodendron), 133
Gloxinia, 26, 31
seeds of, 49
Golden Shower (*Coreopsis tinctoria*), 67–68, 71
Goldenrain-tree (Koelreuteria), 133
Good-luck-leaf, 121
Graft blight, 198
Graftage, 198–219
Grafting, 11, 207–19
in asexual (vegetative) propagation, 53
and cuttings, 11, 12, 132, 207–19
and plastic film, 143
tools for, 210, 227
and top-working of trees, 198ff., 207, 227
Grafts
cleft, 212ff.
saddle, 207, 209
side, 207, 210
splice, 207
veneer, 207
wedge, 207, 219
whip ("tongue"), 207–9
see also Grafting
Gray's Manual, 156
Ground-layering. *See* Layering
Growth regulators, 112, 138

Gypsophila (Babys-breath)
root cuttings of, 133, 136
Gypsophila paniculata, 133n.

Hardy trees and shrubs
cuttings of, 96–115
Halesia (Silver Bell), 133
Hawthorn
seed of, 40
Heath
seed of, 40
Heather
seed of, 40
Helloborus (Christmas-rose), 19
Hemlock
seed of, 40
cuttings of, 154
Heutte, Fred (park superintendent, Norfolk, Va.), 148
Hibiscus syriacus (Rose-of-Sharon)
cuttings of, 116
Hickory
seed of, 18
Hitchhikers (seeds), 17
Holly (Ilex), 133
American (*Ilex opaca*), 154
seed of, 18, 40, 41, 43–44
Hollyhock (*Althaea rosea*), 19
Home Garden, 172
Home Orchid Growing (Rebecca Northen), 36
Honesty (*Lunaria annua*), 19
Honeysuckle
Bush, 98
seed of, 18
Hormodin, 112, 193
Hormones, root-inducing, 138, 186 *passim*
Horse-radish, 195
Hosta (Plantain-lily), 70
House plants
cuttings of, 78–95
Houseleek
Cobweb (*Sempervivum arachnoideum*), 180
Humidity. *See* Moisture; Temperature

Hyacinth, 157
Hydrangea
    cuttings of, 96
Hypericum (St.-Johns-Wort), 133

Ilex (Holly), 133
    seed of, 18, 40, 41, 43–44
Ilex opaca (American Holly), 154
Impatiens, 88
Indian-bean (Catalpa), 133
Iresine (Bloodleaf), 78
Iris
    Bearded, 54, 156
    Japanese, 54
    Tall Bearded, 170–71
Ismene
    seeds of, 17, 21
Ivory-nut Palm
    seeds of, 17

Jasmine
    Winter (*Jasminum nudiflorum*)
    cuttings of, 98
Juniper
    cuttings of, 96, 115
Juvenile forms, 17
Juvenile habit
    retention of, 17

Kalanchoë Daigremontiana, 123
    (*Bryophyllum*) *pinnata*, 123
    verticillata, 123
Knudson, Dr. Lewis, 36
Koelreuteria (Goldenrain-tree), 133
Kolkwitzia
    cuttings of, 104
Kolkwitzia amabilis (Beauty-bush)
    cuttings of, 106

Lantana, 84
Larch
    seed of, 40
Larkspur
    Annual, 19
Lavender, 154

Layering, 12
    air-, 53, 138, 183–84, 188–94
    and graftage, 198
    ground-, 183, 185–87
    mound-, 183
Leaf-bud cuttings, 128–31, 226, 229–30
Leaves
    in asexual (vegetative), propagation, 53
    cuttings of, 53, 121–29
    of seedlings, 17
    see also under Leaf-bud cuttings
Legumes
    seeds of, 18
Lettuce, 29
Leucothoë, 154
    seed of, 40
Liatris (Gay Feather), 19
Life-plant, 121
Lilac, 133, 177
    budding of, 198, 206
    cuttings of, 96, 98
    grafting of, 198, 209
    Meyer's, 150
    purple, 153
    white, 153
Ligurian Harebell (*Campanula isophylla*), 79
Lilium candidum, 162
    hollandicum, 162
    leucanthum, 163
    sulphureum, 161
    umbellatum, 162–63
Lily, 155, 156, 159–63
    Madonna, 54, 160
Lily-of-the-valley, 71
Linden
    seed of, 40
Linum (Perennial Flax), 19
Lobelia, 19, 94
Logan, H. B., 36
Lotus
    East Indian (Nelumbium), 18, 24
Love-in-a-mist, 19
Lunaria annua (Honesty), 19

Maclura (Osage-orange), 133
Magnolia
   cuttings of, 97
   seeds of, 23
   Star (*Magnolia stellata*), 154, 190
Mahonia
   cuttings of, 96
Malling IX (dwarfing understock for Apple), 53
Mamillaria elongata, 215
Maple
   Japanese, grafting of, 210
   seed of, 17, 40
Merck No. 3. *See* Hormodin
Metasequoia glyptostroboides, 154
Milkweed
   seed of, 17
Miracle-leaf, 121
Mock-orange (Philadelphus), 40
Moisture
   and air-layering, 183–84, 194
   and cuttings of hardy shrubs and trees, 96, 109
   and plastic film, 138–43
   and rooting mediums and equipment, 220, 229–30
   and seed germination, 17, 18, 26, 30, 32, 224
   see also Constant mist
Morisia, 134
Mother-of-thousands (*Saxifraga sarmentosa*), 51, 179
Mound-layering. *See* Layering
Mountain-laurel, 26
Mullein (Verbascum), 134
   Greek, 19
Mutations, 127
Myosotis (Forget-me-not), 19
Myrtillocactus geometrizans (Blue Candle Cactus), 214, 215

Narcissus, 155
National Arboretum, 128
Neillia sinensis, 96
Nelumbium (East Indian Lotus), 18, 24

Neomarica Northiana (Apostle-plant), 177
Northen, Rebecca, 36
Notocactus Haselbergi, 217
Nymphaea   Daubeniana   (Dauben Water-lily), 122

Oak
   seed of, 18, 40
Oenothera (Evening-primrose), 134
Offsets, 12
   described, 177
   propagation by, 12, 180
Oleander
   cuttings of, 120
Oöspore, 48
Orchid, 36, 64
   seeds of, 17
Orchids Are Easy to Grow (H. C. Logan and L. C. Cosper), 36
Osage-orange (Maclura), 133
Osmunda fiber, 65–66
Oxydendrum
   seed of, 40

Paeonia moutan (Tree Peony), 218
Pansy (*Viola tricolor hortensis*), 19
Papaver (Oriental Poppy), 134
Parachutes (seeds), 17
Patience-plant, 78
   cuttings of, 83
Paulownia (Empress Tree), 133
   seed of, 17
Peach
   as understock, 199
   "wild," 198
Pear
   budding of, 198
   grafting of, 198, 207
Pelargonium (House Geranium), 81–82, 134
   Mrs. Gordon, 53
Peony, 72–74
   herbaceous, 218
   Tree, 218
   varieties, 19

Peperomia obtusifolia, 126
Perennials
 hardy, 19
 hardy herbaceous, 67–77, 136–37
Perlite, 220
Philadelphus (Mock-orange), 40
Phlox
 division of, 75
 root cuttings of, 132, 134
 varieties, 19
Picea excelsa nana (Spruce, Dwarf), 154
Pickaback-plant (*Tolmiea Menziesi*), 121
Pieris
 cuttings of 96, 98
Pieris japonica, 154
Pilocereus "lanatus cristatus," 217
Pine
 seed of, 17
Pineapple, 20, 178
Plantain-lily (Hosta), 70
Planting
 of biennials, 19
 of hardy annual seeds, 19
 of hardy perennials, 19
 indoors, 26–35
 outdoors, 37–44
 see also Cuttings; Rooting; Seeds
Plastic film. *See* Polythene
Platycodon (Balloon-flower), 19
Pleasant Acres Nursery (New York), 154
Plum
 budding of, 199
Plume-poppy (Bocconia), 133
Poinsettia
 cuttings of, 86–87, 229
Polyanthus
 division of, 76
Polystichum tsus-simense, 58
Polystyrene, 220
Polythene (trade names: Alathon, Duraclear, Pearlon, Polyethylene, Tralon)
 and layering, 183
 and seed germination, 224 *passim*

Poplar
 seed of, 17, 40
Poppy (Papaver)
 California, 19
 Oriental, 23, 54, 134
 Plume, 19
 seeds of, 18, 37
Portulaca
 seeds of, 37
Potato, 156
 Sweet, 197
 White ("Irish"), 197
Potting
 of cuttings, 78–94
 seeds, 26ff.
Primrose
 division of, 54
Primula, 134
Privet
 as grafting understock, 198, 206, 209
Proboscidea (Unicorn-plant)
 fruits of, 17–18, 22
Propagating case
 construction of homemade, 114
Propagation
 asexual (vegetative), 11–12
 sexual, 11
 see also individual means of
Pruning
 Willow's self-, 12–13

Quince, 198

Ragged Robin (Rose), 204
Raspberry
 Black, 177, 181–82
 Red, 177, 182
Rebutia minuscula (Echinocactus minusculus), 35
Retinispora, 154
 varieties, 17
Rhizomes, 12, 170–71
 described, 156
 propagation by, 12

Rhododendron, 26, 128–31, 183
  air-layering of, 183, 193–94
  cuttings of, 97, 154
  leaf-bud cuttings of, 128–31
Rhododendron carolinianum, 129
  decorum, 130
  Kaempferi, 152
  maximum, 129, 131
Rhubarb, 195
Rhus (Sumac, Smoke-tree), 133
Robinia (Rose-acacia, Clammy Locust), 133
Rooting
  mediums and equipment, 220–31
  see also Chapters IV and V; Cut-
    tings; Seeds; Soil; Temperature
Rootone (root-inducing growth regulator), 112
Roots
  in asexual (vegetative), propaga-
    tion, 53
  cuttings of, 53, 78–95, 132–35,
    138–43
  and growth inducers, 138, 186
    passim
  see also Bulbs; Runners
Rootstock, 156, 172–76, 195, 199
Rosa multiflora, 204
Rose
  and budding, 198, 204
  cuttings of, 96, 98
  Dr. Huey (climbing), 204
  and grafting, 198
  Hybrid Tea, 204
  Ragged Robin, 204
  seeds of, 40, 45
Rose-of-Sharon (*Hibiscus syriacus*)
  cuttings of, 116
Runners, 12, 177–79
  described, 177
  propagation by, 12, 177–79

St.-Johns-Wort (Hypericum), 133
Saintpaulia (African-violet), 26, 28,
  31, 52
  cuttings of, 120

Saintpaulia (*cont.*)
  crown cuttings of, 90
  division of, 55–56
  leaf cuttings of, 53, 126–27, 229–
    30
  seed of, 49
  Sir Launcelot, 126
Salix purpurea nana (Dwarf Arctic
    Willow)
  cuttings of, 119
Saloon-plant. *See* Aspidistra
Salsify
  seeds of, 17
Sansevieria trifasciata Laurenti (Snake-
    plant), 53, 59, 60
  leaf cuttings of, 129
Sassafras, 133
Saxifraga aizoon var. (Silver Saxi-
    frage), 180
  sarmentosa (Mother-of-thousands),
    51, 179
Scions, 198 *passim*
Scooping (of bulbs), 157ff.
Scoring (of bulbs), 157
Scotch Broom
  seeds of, 18
Sea Coconut
  seeds of, 17
Sedum (species), 125
Sedum Morganianum (Donkey's Tail),
  123
Seedlings
  budding on, 198, 199, 204
  induced growth of, 45
  leaves of, 17
Seeds (propagation by)
  and air, 18, 32
  of biennials, 19
  defined, 48
  distribution of, 17–18, 22, 23, 24
    (*see also under* Animals; Birds)
  equipment for, 223–25
  floater, 17
  glider, 17
  and graftage, 198
  of hardy annuals, 19

Seeds *(cont.)*
  of hardy perennials, 19
  hitchhiker, 17
  indoor sowing of, 26–35
  and light, 224
  and mixed progeny, 19
  and moisture, 18, 26, 30, 32, 224
  outdoor sowing of, 37–44
  parachute, 17
  of shrubs, 41ff.
  size of, 17
  soil requirements for, 26–35, 37ff.,
    220, 224
  and Sphagnum Moss, 223 *passim*
  and temperature, 18–19, 40
  of trees, 40ff., 198
  two-year, 40
Sempervivum, 177
Sempervivum arachnoideum (Cobweb
  Houseleek), 180
Sexual propagation, 11
Shrubs
  cuttings of deciduous, 116–17
  cuttings of hardy, 96ff.
  root cuttings of, 132
  seed planting of, 41ff.
Silver Bell (Halesia), 133
Skinner, Dr. Henry T., 128
Slosson, Margaret, 48
Smoke-tree (Rhus), 133
Snake-plant (*Sansevieria trifasciata
  Laurenti*), 53, 59, 60
  leaf cuttings of, 129
Soil
  acidity of, 26, 220
  composition of, 26, 220ff.
  drainage of, 220
  and graftage, 199
  and moisture, 18, 26, 30, 32, 220ff.
    (*see also* Constant mist)
  preparation of, 27–34, 37ff., 220ff.
  puddling of, 27, 37
  seeding requirements in, 26–35,
    220, 224
  "sterilization," of, 220

Solomons Seal, 156
Sphagnum Moss, 183, 188ff., 220,
  223 *passim*
Spider-plant (*Chlorophytum elatum*),
  177, 179
Spirea
  cuttings of, 96
Spleenwort
  Ebony (*Asplenium platyneuron*), 48,
    50
  Scott's (*Asplenium ebenoides*), 48,
    50, 51
Spores
  defined, 48
  propagation by, 11, 12, 48–52
Sprinklers (seeds), 18
Sprouting-leaf, 121
Spruce
  Dwarf. *See* Picea
  seed of, 40
Squirting Cucumber
  fruit of, 18
Star-of-Bethlehem. *See* Ligurian
  Harebell
Stephanandra, 133
Stokes-aster (Stokesia), 134
Stokesia (Stokes-aster), 134
Stolons, 12, 177, 181
Stratification (of seeds), 40, 41
Strawberry, 177, 178
Strawberry-begonia, 179
Strawberry-geranium, 179
Suckers
  described, 177
  propagation by, 12, 182
Sumac (Rhus), 133
Sunflower
  seeds of, 18, 22
Sward, Sven (horticulturist), 147,
  154
Sweet Alyssum, 38
Sweet-shrub (Calycanthus), 133
Sweet William (*Dianthus barbatus*), 19
Symphoricarpos Chenaulti
  cuttings of, 104, 106
Syringa Meyeri (Meyer's Lilac), 150

Tamarisk
  cuttings of, 96
Taxus, 220
Temperature
  and artificial light, 229
  and bulbs, 158
  and leaf cuttings, 122, 229
  requirements of in seeding, 18–19, 40
  and rooting mediums, 229–31
  and seed storage, 40
  and shrub-cutting storage, 116, 117
  and soil "sterilization," 220
  and understock storage, 210
Thuja (Arbor-vitae), 17
  cuttings of, 97
Thwing, Walter E., 172, 176
Tolmiea Menziesi (Pickaback-plant), 121
Tomato, 11
Top-working (of trees). See Grafting
Trees
  cuttings of hardy, 96ff.
  deciduous, 13
  fruit, 198ff., 207
  and graftage, 198ff.
  and plastic film, 143
  root cuttings of, 132
  seed plantings of, 40ff.
  top-working of, 207, 227
  see also individual trees
Trichocereus Spachianus, 216, 217
Trillium, 156, 172–76
Trollius (Globe-flower), 134
Trumpet-creeper (Campsis), 133
Tubers, 12, 155–56, 165–70
  described, 155
Tulip, 155, 156, 157
Turquoise Berry
  fruit of, 18

Underdrainage, 98
Understock, 11, 132, 198ff.
Unicorn-plant (Proboscidea)
  fruit of, 17–18, 22

Vassar College, 144, 147
Vegetables (perennial), 195–97
Vegetative propagation. See Asexual propagation
Verbascum (Mullein), 134
Verbascum olympicum (Greek Mullein), 19
Vermiculite, 34, 142, 220 passim
Viburnum
  cuttings of, 96, 97
  seeds of, 41
Viburnum Sieboldi, 154
Vinca, 87
Viola tricolor hortensis (Pansy), 19
Viviparous plants, 121

Wallflower (Cheiranthus Cheiri), 19
Walnut
  seed of, 18, 40
Wandering Jew
  cuttings of, 83
Water lily
  Dauben (Nymphaea Daubeniana), 122
  leaf plantlets of, 121
  seed of, 17
Weigela
  cuttings of, 116, 117
Willow
  Dwarf Arctic (Salix purpurea nana), 119
  Golden Weeping, 118
  root formation of, 12
  seed of, 17, 40
  self-pruning of, 12–13
Wisteria
  cuttings of, 98
  root cuttings of, 133
Witch Hazel
  seed of, 18
Wyman, Donald, 139

Xerophyte, 154

Zygocactus truncatus (Christmas Cactus), 214, 215, 216

ACKNOWLEDGMENTS

The following list shows the sources for photographs used in this book. References are made to pages and the position of the respective photograph: u. upper, c. center, l. lower.

Bishop, George: 25

Brooklyn Botanic Garden: 20, 22 u., 28 u., 45, 46, 85, 117 l., 122, 123, 125, 178 l., 217.

Carroll, M. L.: Drawing 47

Free, Montague: 27 l., 42, 43 l., 44, 52, 61, 62, 78, 81 u., 88, 89, 118 u., 119, 124, 126 l., 127 u., 129, 131, 135 l., 139, 140, 141, 142, 143, 145, 146, 147, 148 u., 149, 150, 151, 152, 153, 155, 156, 157, 158, 159 u., 161 l., 162 l., 163 u., 163 c., 164, 166, 167, 168, 169, 178 u., 181, 182, 185, 186, 187, 188, 189, 190, 191, 192, 204, 205, 206, 209 l., 212, 214, 215, 218, 221, 222, 223.

Gottscho-Schleisner: 94, 95, 126 u., 230 u.

Heutte, Fred: 148 l.

The Home Garden: 35 l., 49, 50, 51, 55, 56, 57, 58, 59, 60, 69, 70, 73 u., 74, 75, 97, 98, 99, 100, 179 u., 228.

Kinney, Malcolm R.: 63, 64, 65, 66, 67, 68, 80, 90, 91, 92, 93, 110, 118 l., 120 u., 120 l., 134, 135, 136, 137, 165, 170, 171, 197 l., 203 l.

The Munson Studio: 101, 102, 103, 104, 105, 199, 200, 201, 202, 203 u.

Purdy, Maud H.: Drawings, 128

Rod McLellan Company: 36

Seabrook Farms: 193, 194.

Skinner, Henry T.: 130

Smith, Richard A.: 72, 73.

Steenson & Baker: 21, 22 l., 23 u., 24, 26, 27, 28, 29, 30, 31, 32, 33, 34, 37, 38, 39, 56 u., 71, 76, 77, 79, 81 l., 82, 83, 84, 86 u., 87 l., 106, 107, 108, 109, 111, 112, 113, 114, 115, 116, 117 u., 117 c., 120 c., 121, 123, 127 l., 159 l., 160, 179 l., 180, 195, 196, 197 u., 207, 208, 209 u., 211, 216.

Thwing, Walter E.: 172, 173, 174, 175, 176.

United States Department of Agriculture: 161 u., 162 u., 163 l., 224, 225, 226, 230 l.

Whiting, John R. (*Flower Grower*): Frontispiece, 23 l., 219.